CARING FOR KIDS

By Harold D. Renshaw

PALO ALTO, CALIFORNIA

Published By

R & E RESEARCH ASSOCIATES
936 Industrial Avenue
Palo Alto, California 94303

Library of Congress Card Catalog Number
81-83610

I. S. B. N.
0-88247-628-9

TABLE OF CONTENTS

ACKNOWLEDGEMENTS

I can't count the children who have helped to write this book. Some of them find their way into anecdotes and examples. Most of them exist in my urge to write a book that tries to help people understand them.

The same is true of staff who have come and gone. I hope they someday see themselves in the book and recognize the tribute I owe them.

A special tribute goes to Patricia Moen, who was in child care until her untimely death in 1978. She was always one of my special people: a person who gave and gave even when she seemed to be able to give no more and really cared for kids.

I also wish to give special thanks to Ms. Barbara Kagel who patiently typed and retyped the manuscript. I would be remiss if I failed to mention Allendale School in Lake Villa, Illinois, where my child care experiences began.

Finally, I wish to thank Alan Spear, Regional Director, Kaleidoscope, for his patient support and suggestions which brought this book to its final form.

INTRODUCTION

If anyone had told me I would be involved in the residential treatment of children when I was in college, I would have never believed them. It was beneath my dignity and not challenging enough. However, if someone had told me I would be engaged in an exciting and challenging job which involved the development of innovative treatment strategies, and that the impact of that work could have profound effect upon the lives of the individuals involved, I would have said, "Wow! Sign me up!"

Both have happened. After four years in child care and about a million experiences, I am still enthusiastic about the business. I have worked in many other branches of social service and each has its challenge and most have more glory, but child care has them beaten by a thousand miles. The kinds of people it attracts, the kinds of experiences it provides, and the impact it can have, make child care the most exciting thing going.

Some will try to dampen this attitude by pointing out that the success rate is very low. It is low, if you want to look at it that way, but the fact that there are any successes at all is owed to the impact of caring people involved in impossible problems.

Child care agencies get their children after everything else has failed. First the family was counseled, then perhaps homemaker services were used. Sooner or later all failed and foster care was utilized and that failed. By the time the child has gone the institutional routes that lead to residential treatment, he or she has been in the system longer than most of the child care workers he or she meets.

You might say that the child has been through years of training. That training has taught these lessons well: you don't trust, you don't love, you don't care, and the world is a place full of manipulators and "manipulatees." Children look for fixed points in their lives around which they can wind their experiences. The parade of placements and menagerie of workers have

vii

not been able to fill that need. Thus, the children remain fragmented, hanging their self-worth on the wind. They can only count on what they have in their grasp and their powers of manipulation.

They have been better trained at this than their mentors. Most of us come from fairly stable environments which we wound our lives around. We are largely unprepared for the hostile world they bring to us. Their training is stronger than ours. That's why we need to be trained. We need to understand that the children behave logically, given their background.

This little book is an attempt to wed the components of human science and humanism. Humanism gives us the attitudes we need to implement what science has given us in the technology of dealing with human problems.

There are no graphs and charts, no math and statistics. At least, there are none visible. This book aims at the core of the child care worker's existence and hopes to dignify and ease the traumas of a very complex and demanding job.

This book emphasizes two elements, you and the child. It stresses that you and the child are both in this together, and that while differences exist, the core of human characteristics is shared. It is working with this core that will make child care effective.

There is a lot of Kaleidoscope in this book. We feel that in our agency we emphasize the core of what child care is. We limit and we structure, but first we care. Caring makes the difference. More systematic programming as is seen in other agencies is not used in Kaleidoscope as an overall methodology.

No matter what system or treatment modality is emphasized, the child and the child care worker remain at the center. It is the interaction that exists between these two main characters, within whatever program that exists, that determines the outcome. Basic child care is the ground upon which residential treatment is built.

How To Use This Book in Training

Different agencies have different training purposes. This book will find its place within any agency's training programs as an orientation to the field.

This book can merely be handed to the new employee and time be given to read it. Better yet, it can be used in group discussion with either new or a mixed group of new and experienced child care workers.

The agency trainer can prepare equations for discussion using chapter subtitles as guides for questions. The trainer should feel free to "flesh out" parts as they pertain to real people and experiences in the agency. Participants should be encouraged to relate principles and examples to their observations within the agency or outside of it.

No one should be reluctant to find fault, contradict or add to the book. It is intended to be a springboard for thought. It has served its purpose if it makes people aware of the child and child care.

While it is intended for child care workers, it can also be used to orient board members and the public to the basic functions of child care.

CHAPTER 1

WHAT'S A NICE PERSON LIKE YOU
DOING IN AN IMPOSSIBLE JOB LIKE THIS?

1. Behavior Is Purposive:

Believe it or not, there is a reason you are involved in child care, and you have your own selfish motivation for being here.

Yes, I said "selfish." You are selfish and somehow or other you are getting your jollies out of working with problem kids. You didn't choose to get your thrills selling flower pots, pumping gas or as a mercenary working in Southeast Asia. For some reason, you wandered into child care and for some reason, it means more to you than a paycheck.

You didn't get into this business for what we can call "primary selfishness." That's what we call it when no other purpose is served than your own, or at least that's all you're really interested in.

Secondary selfishness describes the condition that exists when a person is reinforced for doing something that benefits others. Thus, a person may choose to go into politics to benefit others, or he or she may enter the political arena to amass wealth, fame and power. The first person may reap the benefits of the second, but these goodies are a secondary gain.

In child care, the primary selfishness usually encountered is seen in the person who wants to be loved by children or otherwise reaps goodies from them. This type of person is usually weeded out very quickly by the children. They have their own primary needs to meet.

Secondary selfishness in its varying degrees applies to child care workers. Let's take a look at some of the possibilities.

1. Money. You certainly didn't get into child care to make your fortune. But you might have wanted to do other money things

1

like eat, make car payments, buy a new album or get your teeth fixed. Money might have motivated you to get a job, but it was not the reason you chose child care.

2. _Missionary_. You don't have to be religious to want to bring your message of salvation to the savages. Your message may originate from your own life. At sometime or other, you may have experienced something really important in your life and you want to share this experience with others. Maybe it was a special experience or insight that made a great difference in your life.

Perhaps you learned something in college courses that you want to apply to young people.

Whatever it is, it bears potential for your undoing. When the message is rejected by the savages, you may feel you want to get out and cast your pearls before different swine. In any event, remember how valuable missionaries were to the cannibals.

3. _Therapist_. Like the missionary, the therapist wants to test something. The therapist usually imagines him or herself as bringing something special of himself to the poor souls that will be a dramatic turning point in their lives. For the therapist, the purpose is tied up in who he or she is as well as what he or she has to offer.

The therapist is frustrated because the job does not fulfill this need, the children have learned to manipulate such amateurs and drive them up the wall, and no one presently qualified to be a therapist is working as a child care worker. Therapy (in the traditional sense) and child care are two distinct careers.

4. _Bleeding heart_. Oh, those poor unfortunate waifs! Inspired by an overabundance of sympathy, the bleeding heart attempts to absorb as much satisfaction as possible from loving the unloved. The fact that the kids need more than love and that this type of staff needs the kids more than vice versa is not considered. There is a bleeding heart in all of us, but if we can get it out of our systems, we won't join these poor souls in their inevitable clash with reality and disaster.

5. _Martyr_. This one is always wth us. In fact, martyrdom is a trap many of us fall into (How To Get Burnt-Out. . .). The martyr seeks out failure which is especially sweet after heroic effort in a noble cause.

The martyr usually suffers silently--almost. Someone must find out and appreciate the martyr. The martyr will hang on and be a good child care worker--for awhile. Gradually, the effects

2

of too much pity (self and other) debilitate the martyr and, hero-ically "burnt out," she or he drags off to lick the wounds—sometimes for years.

6. <u>Seeker</u>. Some of us come to find out who we are, what our strengths are and a whole lot of other vague things. There is a certain legitimacy in this motivation, but it isn't enough by itself.

Child care will teach you about yourself and about others and bureaucracies and the evils of society and some good things, too, if you hang on. The goodies you get depend a lot on the goodies you give and your motivation. This brief excursion through the freak show of child care motivation is intended to make you ask yourself some serious questions.

It is right to ask what makes a good child care worker. What is the proper motivation? The answer is not available. Maybe you can tell me. Despite our grandiose trivialities, pretentious illusions and well intended selfishness, it seems that good child care is done and kids are helped.

2. How Are You Similar To The Kids?

If this question doesn't evoke some answers, you are probably in the wrong business.

Think of the origins. We all come from families, no matter how imperfect. At one point, there was a set of things and people that was home and family. There were odors, shadows, voices and all sorts of things that may have grown distorted by time, but the influence and memories stay with us for better or for worse.

Your family helped to form you. It gave you your genetic endowment and the early lessons upon which you built your subsequent learning. You learned trust and mistrust there, love and unlove. It was not all good or all bad for any of us.

Peers added their influence upon you as you grew older. The same thing happened to the children we work with. You learned about sex, money, prejudice and a hundred other things under the influence of peers.

As an exercise, reminisce a little about your friends. Which of them influenced you at eight, ten, fourteen—and how?

We also pick the peers who pick us. A scholarly person seeks intellectual peers. Hikers choose hikers. On it goes. It works that way with you and it works that way with the children we now work with. A certain cultural inbreeding goes on.

You are similar to the children in more ways than you are different from them. The emotions you feel are the same ones they feel. They value attention, so do you. They want to succeed, as you do. They are trapped by some bad habits, so are you. They tell themselves lies, so do you. They fear failure and rejection--is that so foreign?

When you take into account the many ways in which we protect ourselves, want to assert ourselves and want to avoid loneliness, we find that what may seem strange in others becomes more understandable. And when we consider the extremes to which we would go to be "O.K.", nothing much separates "us" from "them."

3. How Are You Different From The Kids?

Differences make life interesting. While acknowledging your part in the flow of the human condition, do not overlook those unending shades of difference which will broaden your horizons if you can understand them, but will fence you out if you can't.

I am not concerned here with those sociological studies which tell us how unjust our systems are, but with the individual experience of that injustice in its daily forms.

Can you understand the type of environment where the only break with the humdrum is stealing something? Can you feel the pressure to drink because it means the difference between acceptance and isolation--at age 12?

How about the fear that Mother's boyfriend will come home with a case of whiskey instead of groceries or that Mother really will blow herself away as she threatened to do when you went to school this morning?

Can you get into the mentality that accepts the moldy smell in the house because that's the way it always is and views people who live in the suburbs as remote as Russians? Can you understand these things and see how they can be part of a life? If so, you can perceive some differences. You are learning.

Nevertheless, the children do differ from what you experienced in childhood.

Family. While the child almost always holds his/her family in high regard, it has not been successful. The child's family rejected him/her, or was at least not successful in withstanding

4

the pressures of society which eventually got the child into placement.

Of course, the particular living style of the child's family may be different from yours. This may be a cultural difference, a difference in socio-economic functioning, or some other difference which you must try to understand and not condemn.

The family difference is important. The child may see the legitimate differences between the "house family" and his/her natural family as a threat. By implication of the system, you are "ok," the child and his/her family is not.

This partially explains why the child may resist getting "sucked into" the therapeutic family. It also explains why the child can be very sensitive about his/her family and may overreact to anything he/she considers a slur against them.

Back home, the child's parents are also feeling like failures. It may seem that some of the parents "don't care," but this is most often a "sour grapes" facade that they wear for you and other representatives of "the system."

"But his mother never writes," you say. "If she cared, she would write." Maybe you would, but do you know that there are reasons why she can still care and not write? Think.

"Her folks promise to come and never show up!" This may be true, but do you understand that even the promise means something and there are reasons why people can't face their failures easily?

Peer group. Everyone is part of one or more systems of social relationships. Most of our children also come from a peer group that helped them achieve their identity.

A great many studies have been done of delinquent peer groups. There is some reason to believe that peer groups exist in hierarchies. At the top are the more organized ones, specializing in fairly sophisticated crimes. At the bottom are kids who are not accepted in the upper layers who loosely band together. Vandalism and avoiding adult control are a characteristic of this group.

We are also attempting to give the child a peer group. The children in placement are giving each other a peer group which is influencing behavior and helping the development of an identity. In placing children, it is important to take this into consideration. We do not deal solely with isolated individuals; we must deal with group influence as well.

That is why it is important to develop a "normalizing environment." As staff, you must realize that you must treat the children as people, not cases, and that what you can do in directing one toward normalization has a "domino effect" on the others.

"Normalizing environment" is an environment that is directed toward adjustment and health. In being so directed, it recognizes peer influence as well as adult roles in directing and caring. It can exist with a token economy or other group program, but it extends beyond such a program. To "normalize" means to make normal, so you can tell it by the atmosphere as well as the results.

The peer group of the child functions like your peer group. The subject matter is different, but the reinforcement and punishment of ideas, behavior and attitudes remains the same. As an exercise, ask yourself how your peers are molding you. What things would you refrain from doing because of your peers' reactions? What things do you do that are influenced by your peers?

Examine also the attitude you and your peers have toward the future. Do you see yourself growing, learning, and developing? We have goals for the children, but what are their goals? Or do they have any goals? Is life something that happens to them and nothing can be done about it?

It is very therapeutic to try to get the children to be self-directive and move away from the "here and now" game playing for personal protection and self satisfaction toward future planning for security and longer range satisfaction.

This can be done through creative scheduling (see fourth chapter). It can also be done in the intimate "rap" that sometimes occurs in those unplanned moments when mind meets mind.

4. How Do The Kids See You?

When you start out in child care, you want to think that you are going to be seen in heroic dimensions by the children. Actually, it's quite different.

The children see you as an angel. A simple being boding good things for them. You're an easy mark. Many of the kids have met missionaries before, taken the goodies they offered. Afterwards, they left the poor angels by the wayside with tarnished haloes and shattered dreams.

But you might have the tougher stuff it takes to really be an angel and then you'll really earn your wings.

The kids can see you as a demon (if you're a really good angel). As a demon, you are frustrating at the moments when something needs to be frustrated. You frustrate the runaway attempt, the attempt to "con" someone, the big "rip off" or the attempt to be irresponsible.

The beauty of being a demon is that you at least can be the angel you once wanted to be. If they see you as this kind of demon, they will see you as fair, firm and consistent, and if you ever get through to them, they will be the kind of demon you are.

The worst way you can be characterized in the kids' minds is "just passing through." If we tend to categorize kids, kids also categorize us, and "just passing through" is a category they most often put us in.

They've seen us before, the eager idealists whose promises flower so quickly and wither even quicker. First of all, they see you that way, one of the innumerable parade of names and faces that have and will pass before their eyes. If you're going to make a difference, you are going to have to fight that label: "just passing through."

There is only one way to fight that classification. Stay. Dig your teeth and nails in, say goodbye to your dreams of wealth and fame, promise yourself that you'll build that empire next year and STAY.

Get spit in your face, a tooth knocked out, sugar in your tank and STAY.

Give up sleeping well, waste a lot of time, tear out your guts and STAY.

Cry like a baby, alienate your friends, forget what day it is, get chewed out for not doing enough (or doing too much) and STAY.

5.   Now ask yourself some serious questions.

"Like what?"

Like: Why bother? It's a tough job, it doesn't pay well, you don't get credit for it and the supervisor just yelled at you.

Why bother? The kids don't appreciate you.

Why bother?

Ask yourself some more questions.

"Like what?"

I don't know, they're your questions.

CHAPTER 2

WHAT MAKES SAMMY RUN?

There was a loud knocking on the door. Sammy, age thirteen, looked away from the T.V. and across the dark and cluttered room to the window. Through the flimsy curtains he could see two figures, one a lean white man in blue jeans and a small blond goatee; the other was a woman in a blue pantsuit. She was young and black, but had straightened hair and lots of rings and other jewelry.

He looked back at the T.V. The vertical hold was losing its grip on a twenty year old western, but it was the reality Sammy preferred at the moment. "If I keep quiet," he thought, "if I just keep quiet."

The knocking came louder the second time. "Mrs. Nunez! Sammy! We know you're in there. Answer the door."

Momma stirred in the bedroom. "Sammy, who's at the door?" Sammy said nothing. Better to be quiet.

Sammy heard Momma sit up, cough and light a cigarette.

here "Mrs. Nunez, it's me, Miss Cantrell. Mr. Lawrence and I are ~~hear~~ for Sammy! Open up!"

"Sammy, get the door. Let 'em in."

Without a sound, Sammy got off the couch and darted into the bathroom. The window there would afford him the exit he needed.

As he made his way to the window past the corroded sink and the assorted underwear and socks, he thought "Why can't they leave me alone? Them damn social workers never leave me alone."

It started a long time ago. It seems like a social worker has always been a part of the family. There was Mr. Swan, the fat guy who always seemed so jolly. He laughed all the time. He even laughed when he took Juanita away when Sammy was just a little

9

guy. Sammy couldn't remember why he did it. She was his oldest sister. Sammy remembers everyone crying and screaming and Mr. Swan acting like it was funny and the cops were there pushing everyone around. Juanita never came back. Sammy thinks she's dead.

The baby's gone too. Momma's boyfriend hit her too much, so one day, a few months ago, Miss Cantrell came by and bundled her up and went out the door. Momma didn't scream. She just sat in the big chair and stared at her feet. She didn't fight anymore.

Sammy's first worker was Kevin Clark, a tall black guy who was everyone's buddy. He told Momma, "Hey Lady, nobody gonna take your kids away; I'll hang in there witcha!" He put Sammy in Howell House two months later and by the time Sammy split from there, good old Kevin Clark had moved on, taking his collection of empty promises with him.

Then Miss Cantrell came along. She is such a fine lady with all that jewelry and her clothes. She always talks to Momma like she's a kid and she walks into the house like a queen among some pigs. Sammy hates all the social workers, but they are all wrapped up in Miss Agnes Cantrell. She took the baby, and, for the second time, she's trying to take Sammy.

Sammy got to the bathroom window. He tugged, but it wouldn't open at first. Finally, he managed to pry it up. Then it came too fast as something seemed to snap. It shattered all over Sammy. He didn't check for cuts, he angled his wiry body out the opening and just as freedom seemed to be there, the social worker with the goatee grabbed him by the back of the neck.

Sammy fought and struggled, but the goateed man was too strong. "You crap eat'n turkey, I'll kill you! I'll kill you! I'll kill you! Let go me so I can kick ya cross-eyed!"

Miss Cantrell was inside the bathroom now and she tiptoed her way through the broken glass. "Hold him good, Mr. Lawrence. Now bring him to the car."

Without saying a word to Momma, Miss Cantrell walked past her in the bathroom doorway and out through the front door.

By the time she reached the car, Mr. Lawrence had slammed Sammy up against it and had him in a choke hold with a hammerlock.

"Ouch, you're hurting me, you SOB!" Sammy yelled, "Let me go!"

10

"Put him in the back seat, Mr. Lawrence," Miss Agnes Cantrell said as she opened the back door of her new green Buick, "but hang on to him!"

Mr. Lawrence shoved him onto the floor, face down. Then he got in and still holding the hammerlock, he put his knee in Sammy's back. It hurt, but Sammy was silent. The tears were gone and he just closed his eyes and lay still as Miss Agnes Cantrell started her car and drove East on Market. He ached.

The thought passed through Sammy's head that his mother was watching with tears in her eyes, screaming, like she did when Juanita was taken, but he knew she wasn't screaming or looking or anything. She probably was lighting another cigarette and looking at the broken glass on the floor in the bathroom.

It seemed like almost an hour of bumping, stopping and turning corners before someone spoke. It was Miss Agnes Cantrell who broke the silence (she always was the one). "Sammy, how do you feel now?"

("The bitch doesn't deserve an answer.")

"Sammy, how do you feel? Don't you think it was stupid to run from Daleglen Training School like that? You should feel pretty stupid. I would if I were you."

"You are stupid, Bitch!" Sammy exploded.

The hammerlock tightened. "You don't talk to ladies like Miss Cantrell that way." (At least Mr. Lawrence had something to say.) "Apologize!"

Sammy bit his lip. He wasn't going to let anyone know how much he hurt.

"No Mr. Lawrence, I don't expect anymore than that out of Sammy. He won't appreciate what we do for him now. He's too angry now and that's understandable. Later, he'll thank us."

The floor of the car was too clean. Sammy's nose was pressed against a brand new rubber floor mat. New rubber smell, not a bit of dirt in sight. The two social workers talked on in tones that he was supposed to hear, but in words that ignored him. Sammy had heard it before a hundred times. On they talked until their words were just more car noises.

He remembered Beaver. Miss Agnes Cantrell had put him in Daleglen about a month after she put Sammy there last summer.

11

One night, they had split out the side door of the old Bellarmy cottage for a midnight swim in the lake.

"Hey, Sammy, see that old innertube over there?" Beaver said as he threw off his pajama bottoms. "That's old black ass Cantrell."

"Let's get her," Sammy had said. "I'm gonna kick her ass good--give her what she needs!"

Beaver got really wild then. "No you don't until I give her what she needs first." With that, he jumped on the innertube and started fighting it like a wild animal.

Sammy had never seen anything like it. Beaver pounded that tube furiously, screaming so loud that Sammy knew the whole place must be awake by then. Sammy could hardly tell what Beaver was screaming. His voice was loud, high pitched and every other word seemed to be choked with anger and tears.

When the staff finally waded into the lake and pulled Beaver out, the innertube lay deflated on the lake surface. Beaver was so upset that he had to go to the infirmary and get a shot.

The next day, they say that the innertube had been bitten into shreds. Sammy now knew why Beaver was so furious at Miss Agnes Cantrell. "I ain't gonna take it out on no innertube; I'll wait for the real thing," Sammy thought as he closed his eyes again on the Buick floor.

"Want up Sammy?" Mr. Lawrence said. Sammy hadn't noticed that the car had stopped. He smelled food, but his stomach was upset.

"We bought you a 'burger'," said Miss Agnes Cantrell with that you-owe-me-again tone of voice ". . . and fries," added Mr. Lawrence who seems to be learning to be another Miss Agnes Cantrell.

Sammy struggled up. Mr. Lawrence let go of the hammerlock. Sammy's arm dropped like a dead weight. He couldn't feel anything in it. With his right hand he reached out for the burger, received it and then held it in his lap.

"Now, isn't that better?" Miss Agnes Cantrell said more than asked. "We'll be at Daleglen in a few minutes. You know, the Department has been paying them to keep a bed for you these three weeks since you ran away. I hope you appreciate all we've done for you; all the people who are concerned about you."

("Hell, Bitch, If I preciated all you say I oughta I wouldn't have time to fart!")

He sat in sullen silence as they drove up the big four lane highway. They had left the city behind. His mother was gone now. She was probably down at Slick's Bar by now. She'll be o.k.

Trees seemed to move by like tall shadows. Sammy rested his face on his left hand which served as a buffer between his head and the window. Three weeks ago, he had seen this scenery the other way, riding in an old Plymouth with the minister.

"Are you in trouble, boy?" The minister had asked as he let Sammy into his rusty old Plymouth. "Not anymore!" Sammy had said. "I was taken up here by the Latin Kings 'cause I blew the whistle on 'em. Lucky they didn't kill me, I guess. Anyhow, I'm goin' back to see my momma--see she's alright."

"You believe in the Lord, boy?" The minister asked. Before Sammy could answer, the minister opened a paper bag and grabbed half a sandwich and took a big bite out of it.

"You believe, boy?" He said again without giving Sammy a chance to reply. Sammy was eyeing the sandwich.

"Oh, I go to church sometimes," Sammy replied, hoping against experience that that would end the topic.

For half an hour, the minister munched on apples, french fries, potato chips and other things and told Sammy about what the Lord had done for him. Finally, the minister pulled into a service station to get something to drink. "Wait here boy; I gotta get me a Coke. I got a powerful thirst, talkin' 'bout the Lord."

Sammy wished he could have seen his face when he got out of the service station. He had thrown the minister's Bible out the window and split down the old highway in the tired old Plymouth.

Three or so miles down the road, Sammy got out of the car and continued to thumb his way home.

By now, Miss Agnes Cantrell was driving down the long lane into Daleglen Training School. He saw them out on the east diamond, playing ball. He looked for Beaver, but he was nowhere in sight.

Up to the administration building the too clean Buick glided, then parked. Soon they were standing by the front desk.

"Sammy's back!" Miss Cantrell trilled triumphantly for everyone to hear.

"Well, Sammy boy, we missed you!" Sammy turned around to see Al Tyrone, the cottage supervisor behind him, leaning in the doorway.

Al was a good guy. "He can't help it, he musta been born a staff," Beaver used to say. Beaver said Al was o.k., "but don't never get too close. He's staff no matter what he seems like."

Al used to sit by Sammy's bed at night and talk to him. Sammy would usually ignore him; pretend to be asleep. Sometimes Al would pretend to believe him and talk about Sammy as if he were talking to someone else in the room.

"Old Sam's had a hard time today," he would say. "Slugged me, or at least tried to. If I hadn't dodged him, he mighta laid me out cold. But ol' Sammy wasn't really mad at me. No sir, ol' Sam is just mad at the world. I just happened to be handy. Some day, Ol' Sam's gonna quit being mad and I won't have to worry about my head flyin' off my shoulders."

Sammy never did know what Al was talking about, but he knew that Al understood him and liked him. He wished his momma could say things like that.

"Well, Sam," Al said, "Let's go back to the cottage. The air around you keeps tellin' my nose that you need a bath."

"Goodbye, Sammy. You stay this time," Miss Agnes Cantrell said without looking at him. "Could we see Mr. Simons a minute before we go?"

Simons was the Daleglen social worker. Sammy knew that she and Simons would talk about him, using all those words social workers use. The next day Simons would call him out of the cottage and try to talk to him like a friend and Sammy would get angrier and angrier because it was an act and he'd fallen for it too many times. "Maybe tomorrow I'll slug him in the gut and laugh my ass off!"

The cottage was the same. The chairs were neatly placed around the table. The rec room was clean, but the pool cues were gone. Staff probably locked them up because someone had used them in a fight.

"Your room has a new guy. His name is Tony Bartholomew. We call him 'Bart.'" I think you'll like him o.k.," Al explained.

14

"Where's Beaver?"

"Ah, that's the bad news. He went crazy the day after you split. He took a pool cue after me. He broke a coupla windows out and we had to grab him. He calmed down a little but when we weren't watchin', he got out and clobbered Mr. Simons with a tree limb. Broke out a tooth, maybe two. Ol' Simons was out cold when I got there and Ol' Beaver was kickin' him."

"Well, we called the hospital and got Beaver over there and Miss Cantrell was called. She decided to place him someplace else. Never told us where he went."

"What happened to Simons?" Sammy asked.

"Oh, he got over it, but nobody ever figured out why Beaver attacked him. You got any ideas, Sam?"

"Nope."

That night, Sammy lay down gladly in the bed. He could hear the frogs on the lake and the other country noises. It wasn't like the city. Too quiet. He fell asleep before Al could come in for his nightly routine.

The next thing he knew, the light was coming through the window and he could hear the guys getting up. He glanced at Bart's bed. It was empty. The sheets were gone. "So, Ol' Bart's a bedwetter. That means the room is always going to stink. Either urine or disinfectant. They're both bad. No one wants a bedwetter in the room."

Next thing he knew, Yeats was standing in the doorway. "So you're back! Have they told you what your punishment is yet? Well, starting today, you wash the basement floor everyday for three weeks. A day for a day! Now, get up!"

Yeats was the supervisor. Fair, but tough. He thought Al was too lenient. Sammy liked him, but he also hated him. He had felt almost glad to be back before. Now, he wasn't sure.

Sammy crawled out of bed, grabbed a towel, went to the bathroom. Yeats was there already, yelling at George and Bob for something or other. With Yeats watching, Sammy had to wash, but the resentment was clutching in his throat already.

The day went by slowly. School, teachers, lunch, scrubbing the basement floor. Glen stood over him. Glen was the most irritating of all staff. He never let a kid say or do anything without some sarcastic remark. He never seemed to get close to any kids; he just seemed to put in his time, doing what he was told to do by Al or Yeats.

Al was off that day. Sammy could have used him there. He was the only one he could talk to.

At 4:00 in the afternoon, Mr. Simons called Sammy to his office in the administration building.

"Well, hello, Sammy. I'm glad you're back. Have a seat." He sat there rocking back in his chair, a big white bowled pipe protruding from beneath his hooked nose and uneven bushy mustache. There was silence for a minute.

"Well . . .?" Mr. Simons asked as if Sammy had not finished a sentence.

Sammy was silent.

"Well, are you glad to get back with us?"

"What do you think?"

"You sound angry."

("There he goes again! Social work talk.")

"What did you do to Beaver?"

"That's Beaver's business. We're talking about you."

"I don't want to talk to you at all. Beaver's my friend and what did ya do with him? Tell me!"

"You are afraid we might hurt you or send you away. Is that it?"

"Where's Beaver?"

"He's safe."

"Where's Beaver, you turd!"

"He's safe."

With that, Sammy jumped up out of his chair, knocking it over. He felt like killing Mr. Simons. The only thing that held

16

him back was—well, he didn't know what. Without further delay, he knocked open the office door and stomped out.

"Come back, Sammy." Simons yelled from his office without leaving his chair. Sammy went back to the cottage.

The guys were out at recreation. Sammy went to his room. Glen came down the hall and told him to go out to play ball.

"Shove it!" Sammy said.

Glen said, "No, play it," as Sammy kicked open the front door and ran toward the ball diamond.

To get there, Sammy had to pass the garage where the agency cars were parked. Looking inside, he saw someone dart behind the green station wagon. "Who's there?" He half whispered into the dark.

"That you Sammy? Come in."

"Whatcha doin'?"

"Bart and me are hot wirin' the green wagon. We're headin' for California." It was George.

"Gotcha, man. Count me in!"

It wasn't long before the green wagon backed out of the stall and gears grinding, with Sammy in the driver's seat, went jerkily down the lane and pulled out on Highway 24, heading West.

"Turn the radio on!" George demanded. George and Bart were in the front seat with Sammy fighting over the radio station.

"Cool it! I can't drive with you fightin' like a coupla jerk-offs."

"Who made you boss, Sammy?" George screamed.

"Yeah, this was our idea, you just came along!" Bart chimed in.

Hardly two miles down the road found the car first going from curb to center line and finally swerving from curb to curb. The speed increased as panic set in and the lady and her daughter coming home from Brownies saw only a big green flash into their lane before the cars met head on and then fell side by side into the ditch.

17

In what seemed to be only a minute, Sammy looked up from the grass into the face of a highway patrolman.

"You lie still, son. You're hurt."

"Where's Beaver?" Sammy said, then everything seemed to get a muddy grey.

The next thing Sammy knew he was in a hospital room. Mr. Simons was sitting beside him reading a _Time_ magazine.

"Well, you're awake. How do you feel?"

"I don't know. I think my leg hurts."

"You broke it. That's the end of running for awhile."

"Where's George? Where's Bart?"

"Bart's back at Daleglen. George is not so lucky."

"Is he hurt?"

"I'm afraid he didn't come out so lucky. He's in surgery."

"Is he gonna die?"

"No, but I'm afraid it is serious. He has a concussion and other head injuries. I wish it wasn't necessary to tell you, but two others were hurt in the crash. A mother and her little girl in the car you hit are in intensive care."

"Oh man, I'm in real trouble now!"

"Yes, Sammy, I can't help you much this time. We're discharging you from Daleglen. It was bad enough when you ran by yourself, but this time you took some others with you. You are too dangerous for our program. We can't take such risks."

Sammy noticed the cast now. It went from his knee down to his foot. He couldn't listen to Simons. He looked at his cast. He looked to his left at the venetian blind which illuminated stripes of dust across the floor.

"Sammy, Miss Cantrell will be here tomorrow. She'll help you out. When you get out of the hospital, she'll try to place you somewhere else, but you'll probably wind up in a reformatory. Face it now."

"Does Momma know?"

"Miss Cantrell told her."

"What did she say?"

"Nothing."

CHAPTER 3

WHAT IS A FAMILY, ANYHOW?

Sammy was jolted awake by the train coming to a stop. Lights in the train came on and people, gathering packages, coats and little children, crowded into the aisle.

"Randolph Street," the pudgy gray faced man in blue said to no one at all as he walked past Sammy and into the next car.

Sammy grabbed the green suitcase and the paper sack from the floor and pushed into the stream of people following the conductor.

Outside the train, there were crowds of people all over. At least half of them had Christmas packages, Sammy observed. He felt a kind of pride. He had one, too. It wasn't big. It was a bottle of wine, in a fancy gold box, and that was in red and green wrapping paper. There was even a card he made himself.

"Crazy!" Sammy laughed out loud to himself. He was thinking of that wine. Doug had purchased it for him. He helped Sammy wrap it.

"Sam," he said, "This is good wine. Your mamma's gonna love it. Tell her to sip it slow--slightly chilled."

"Momma'd never had such good wine," Sammy thought to himself, "She'll be so happy!"

Sammy didn't know a lot about wine, but he knew his mother drank wine and she would certainly like a $6.00 bottle!

Doug had trusted Sammy. This was something Sammy had experienced over nine months. He had run four times and had been returned three. He returned on his own the last time.

Sammy had grown to like the group home. He had a lot of fun there. More than that, he had begun to feel comfortable there. He even felt good about feeling bad because Sandra got pregnant

20

and lost the baby. Sandra was like a sister and he didn't want her to be hurt.

There was the long walk past the flower sellers, the newsstands, and the phonebooths. Then the cold street, dark and damp with the rushing crowds. Sammy hoped he would remember the bus routes.

"Sammy! Sammy!" It was Sammy's mother! Sammy turned around. He hadn't expected her.

She was coughing as she came up the ramp toward Sammy. She had a cigarette in her hand and her old imitation fur coat looked kind of ratty. But Sammy had never seen anything so wonderful in his whole life. "Momma came to meet me!" he thought, as with tears in his eyes, he ran back to meet her.

1. Family Styles:

When we talk of styles, we are not implying that everyone or anyone fits neatly into one style or another. These styles are used to give us a conceptual framework to understand the processes of family interaction which result in what we will call "normal" or "abnormal" life styles in children.

It may be over-simplified, but it is possible to see the family as a people-factory. Some families produce people who hold jobs, don't get in trouble with the law, enjoy other people and like to live. On the other hand, we find that there are people who can't hold jobs, mistrust and aren't trusted, and, in general, feel miserable with life.

When we look at families, we find that it is unusual to see a maladjusted child from a well put together family.

But there is a positive element to the study of these styles. They show child care workers what children expect from adults and they also point to the therapeutic value of a group living style which promotes healthy communication, feelings about self, and the skills of successful adjustment.

For lack of better classifications, let's assume that families fall into three classifications. These are autocratic, laissez faire and democratic. They are types or styles, not neat boxes into which all families fall. Look upon them rather as styles which may be used to classify any parent/child relationship at a random point in time.

The authoritarian style has one parent (sometimes both) who directs the family. Most communication comes from this parent to the family members and communication flows upward only on command.

Discipline is inflexible according to the needs of the head, not the needs of the members. Any violation is seen as a personal affront upon the head and his control. As a result, discipline emphasizes control over correction and learning.

It is implied in this family style that the head does not trust the members. Their ideas are not considered and in turn, they get used to not having any. Members also feel that they have little responsibility for the family and as a result, only minimal allegiance is felt for the family as a whole by any member except the autocrat(s). Security is high, but self reliance is low.

The pure democratic style, on the other hand, has a head who feels that his or her main responsibility is to maintain participation at the highest levels possible. When direction is needed, it is given, but decisions are made with as much participation as possible.

Trust is given as each member is able to take responsibility. The head sees to it that responsibility fits the capacity of each member. As a result, the children in this family style mature evenly and generally encounter few crises that they cannot successfully handle.

In the democratic style family, a sense of group identity is achieved and serves as a strength for each member. The family group will rush to the aid of any member in trouble. After the members of the family have grown, they still remain a family.

Discipline in the democratic style family is generally fair, but firm. It is more likely to be suited to the needs of the offender than to the needs of the head or other members. Offenses may be seen as a threat to the family unit, but because of the participative nature of this family style, offenses are much less likely to occur in the first place. This family style is high on security and high on self reliance.

In the laissez faire family style, the family resembles a crowd more than a group. Family ties are not as important as friendship or work ties. Occasionally, the head with assert some autocratic type of control, but this is generally unpredictable. The message seems to be that "everyone does their own thing" except every now and then when someone must be coerced, nagged or bribed into doing something for the group.

Respect is low in this group because security is almost non-existent. Children feel almost at sea, alone in an unpredictable world. They can't count on guidance to help unless some family member feels like it.

Discipline is generally inconsistent. It may be harsh or it may be mild. It often takes the form of whatever act will immediately reinforce the discipliner by stopping the irritating behavior. You can usually hear this family yelling from about two blocks away.

When a crisis occurs, these family members may pull together briefly or they may just do what they can to avoid it.

As you can surmise, the laissez faire family style produces low security and low self reliance.

Remember, these are broad, general categories which do not cover every family situation. In fact, no family fits any one of them. They are styles which are viewed in the extreme to provide a framework for understanding family differences and some of their effects.

2. <u>The Ideal Family</u>:

As a social unit, the family is presumed to be all things to all people. This is impossible. The family is the basic unit of society, but it is not society. It is important that we not fall into the trap of believing the family is more than it really is. The family is the first learning environment, the main support system while we grow up, and the model for future social interactions. The ideal family has important tasks to perform, but it should not be expected to be everything.

The ideal family has what we will call "unconditional care." This means that you don't earn your way into it. The family isn't a social club with entrance requirements and expulsion criteria. The family keeps you. The family welcomes you back. The family responds to your needs and does the best it can for you.

Unconditional care does not mean that you are praised for whatever you do. You can get the "cold shoulder" if you do something that irritates people. No family should guarantee you "unconditional positive regard" at all times. People do not learn without some feedback, and part of it is going to be negative.

The family also does not sacrifice its health or existence to your idiosyncrasies. Unconditional care does not imply that you are allowed to destroy the unit. As with any organic unit,

23

any serious threat to its survival will cause it to eject the threat.

The family cannot allow you to hurt yourself. As part of the family, you must contribute or at least not detract from it. If you are hurting yourself, the family can be expected to do something about it. First, the members will respond internally. If that doesn't work, rather than see you hurt, the family will seek external intervention.

The family provides a safe environment for children. It is safe both physically and psychologically. Standards are maintained for health and physical safety and limits are maintained for psychological safety.

3. Spheres of Responsibility:

It is easy to determine the needs and limits of physical safety and health. However, the broader question of spheres of responsibility (SOR) requires judgement and flexibility.

A SOR is that area, physical and psychological, for which a given individual can be given or can take responsibility. To put it differently, we individualize according to what can be handled. A baby cannot take any responsibility, so the baby isn't given any. The baby isn't trusted, isn't held responsible, isn't asked to explain, and is beneath forgiveness.

The older adolescent, on the contrary, is able to be responsible for cooking, cleaning, driving the family car, behavior on dates, and all sorts of things. Why? Because the adolescent has demonstrated the ability to handle these things, and, most importantly, the ability and willingness to accept the natural consequences of mistakes and mishaps in these areas.

How are SORs determined? These decisions are made objectively and by subjectively informed decisions.

Objectively, a person is legally, physically, educationally, and experientially able or not able to do certain things. A fifteen year old may be able to drive a car, but the law dictates some restrictions upon this act as do insurance companies.

Subjective judgment is not necessarily arbitrary. The parenting person makes a judgment that a certain activity is beyond the SOR of a particular child. This is usually based upon past experience--or lack thereof--with a particular child.

24

Example: you have heard that a local store is a place where teenagers buy drugs. Now, a child in the family wants to go for a walk in that direction at every opportunity. In the parenting role, you have to decide whether this is the SOR of this child. He or she may be allowed to go anywhere else in town, but not there.

Finding the boundaries of the SOR requires knowledge, experience, intuition and risk. This last element is very important. Some people forget that children grow by taking some risks. If risk taking did not occur, no baby would ever sit up, eat alone or walk.

Finally, establishing SOR's means being willing to take some flack yourself. It would be easy to have the same rules for everyone, so that you would never have to defend your decisions. In essence, that would demand that no one grows and no one is different. Of course, this also dictates that those who do need to expand their SOR's do so by rebellion.

4. **Family Roles:**

Limits in the family include roles that people acquire. All roles are defined by their function. Someone budgets the money, someone consoles the sorrowful, someone does the heavy work, someone plans the meals. Not that roles are rigid. They are mixed. From time to time, the heavy work person may plan meals, for instance, but in the final analysis, he or she will not look upon that as a role function until two things happen: Until he or she sees it as his or her role; and until other people in the family expect it of him or her and reinforces its continued performance.

Deviant roles are sometimes reinforced. This creates the expectation that so and so will get into trouble and be the black sheep. We occasionally meet these children in placement. They usually quit being deviant when they lose the role reinforcement.

5. **The Therapeutic Family Environment:**

Family feelings need to be created in group living. Especially needed is a feeling of togetherness which you would expect to be lacking in a diverse group. The general rules for doing this are:

1. Create pride in the group's identity.

2. Design situations in which the group must pull together.

3. Design competitions with other groups.

4. Reinforce mutual care.

25

5. Make individual happy (and even sad) events occasions to share with the group.

6. Make group decisions about group activities and concerns.

6. The Family in Continuity:

In the beginning, the child experiences the family as a place of safety. The outside world is only safe when the family's protection covers the child as he ventures into it. It is with this security that the normal child enters the community, carrying the self-confidence and security the home has taught.

In later years, the family serves as a fixed point around which the members can rally and a sheltered refuge to heal your wounds. This continues as time goes on.

Basic social skills, annoying habits and endearing traits are learned at home during the first few years of life. Basic attitudes toward self, others and life in general are also learned during these first few years. Later, experiences can change things for better or for worse, but the early experiences are formative and their influences are rarely erased.

(The argument still rages between the geneticists and the environmentalists. Their battles are interesting, but not highly relevant, especially when you realize that child care presumes that environmental changes can make a significant difference.)

The family teaches through three methods: Reinforcement, punishment, (and ignoring) and modeling.

The power of modeling influences has been greatly underestimated and misunderstood in the past. If the child observes someone of the same sex who has prestige or power consistently performing a particular role, it is highly likely that the child will incorporate this role into him or herself.

Sex role expectations are formed in childhood. A male not only learns what masculinity is (for him), but also learns what females are (for him). Sexual chauvinism begins rather early.

Emotional responses are also learned through early modeling. What do you do when frustrated? First of all, you do what you've seen done by important models. You retreat, you plan, you cuss, you break something, you do whatever you've seen done by model(s) in your life.

The second determinant of your reactions is the contingency pattern which has existed for you in the past. For instance, you put a coin in the Coke machine, push the button and nothing happens. What do you do? In the past, you flipped the coin return lever and the coin came back. If that doesn't work you try the next thing that has worked: You hit it. Next you kick it. Etc. Etc.

Social situations work the same way. The behavior that gets you acceptance, approval and/or results will be repeated in similar situations. Behaviors that are punished or get no results soon disappear.

7. Family Pathology:

It is probably safe to say that no child from a healthy family is placed in residential treatment. In other words, no one messes up his or her own life as a solo do-it-yourself project. We all need help to be "sane" and we all need help to be "crazy." It's hard to go it alone.

A family is a fragile and sometimes accidental-incidental system. The influences of social inequities, personal and interpersonal dysfunctions, financial pressures and a myriad of factors seem to compete to weaken and destroy it. The long term poor family seems to be the most vulnerable to the manipulations of federal, state and local agencies. At the same time, they are dependent upon these agencies, they are frustrated and debased by them.

The result is a feeling of helplessness and worthlessness. When the children are removed, parents sometimes feel that the children have been sacrificed to the impersonal gods of the middle class agencies.

If you take a look at Sammy's mother back in chapter two, you may get a glimpse of how she had resigned herself to this process.

This is not to say that children should not be removed. It is the bitter reality that some situations cannot be saved and that--at least for the time being--children must be separated from a deteriorating situation.

If we remove the child, it is not saying that we cannot return the child. If we cannot return the child, it is not to say that the ties cannot be maintained or restored.

It takes some sensitivity to understand that the parent may need to be prodded to accept the idea of return or contact.

27

Agencies stand in middle class, with awesome miles between them and parents. Can the parent give the child the "goodies" that the agency does? Probably not.

Yet almost every child in placement would gladly throw the middle class existence of child care back in your face if he or she could realize that dream behind the plea: "When can I go home?"

8. Creating the Family:

To create a family atmosphere, the adults must make the commitment. The commitment is to do the hard work it takes to turn a bunch of individuals into a real group.

First of all, put your staff image in the back of your head for a while. Be willing to do _with_ as much as _for_. Play _with_ the kids, cook _with_ the kids, plan fun things _with_ the kids. When they see you are with them, they will respond more with you. Carry this into everything you do.

Make the family environment warm and secure. Warmth in the environment implies a lot of good feelings generated by people giving and receiving positive "strokes." It is a state of reciprocity in which you give to me and I give to you. When I am sad, you notice and somehow let me know you care. When I do something correctly, you praise me. When I tell a joke, you laugh.

All of these little things bring warmth, and they are all too varied and individual to list, and they grow out of knowing the individual, not reading a list. A well placed bit of sarcasm may be the right thing for Marie, but Joe needs a friendly punch on the arm.

"Different strokes for different folks."

BUT STROKE!

Security is dealt with in the chapter on structure and consistency. It is the basis for warmth. Warmth makes sense only in a secure environment. Think about it.

28

CHAPTER 4

STRUCTURE, CONSISTENCY

1. Where Does Health Come From?

"I went to visit my brother's family last week," Jerry said, "I don't understand how his kids got so . . . a . . . healthy!"

After a time on the front line, Jerry had forgotten how "normal" kids act. After a time at the job of child care, you can be as amazed at health as you originally were at the extremes of misbehavior.

Where does this kind of appropriate behavior come from? Why are some children well behaved, good humored and generally adjusted while others are trapped into maladaptive patterns which lead to placement?

Ruling out the rare cases of organic disturbance, the cause of behavior disorders seem to come from disorderly families. It is not the one-time trauma that disturbs the balance. It is usually the effects of big and little insecurities strung out over years when a secure environment was so desperately needed.

Think about it a minute. Our lives are built upon some kind of security. We have confidence because we have learned to count on reality, especially the significant people in our lives. Because we are secure, we can risk and grow.

As children, our parents made our world secure. We could count on them for food when we were hungry, warmth when we were cold, a smile when we were good and a consequence for other actions.

Gradually, with love and discipline, our world became secure. We would not be abandoned or hurt and we learned where limits were. We accepted limits because they were secure for us. We did not push the limits once they were established, and we quickly learned to accept new limits and expectations because our past experiences made us feel secure in reality and confident in our ability.

2. Schedules:

Health, as we use it here, comes from security. The children who come to us have experienced very little of it. While we must extend security in the less tangible realm of care and concern, security will not be experienced until the total environment can be counted upon.

One essential is to provide a schedule of daily and weekly activities that can be relied upon. Another important item is time defined goals that can be accomplished in a relatively short time.

Each day has demands that define schedules by necessity. School and work demands tell us when we should arise, at least in some minimal way. Allowing adequate time for clean up, bed making, breakfast, etc., further gives definition to the morning schedules.

Other scheduling is more artificial. A stable time for the evening meal is a prerequisite for a secure environment. Homework time, chores, group recreation and even time to be alone can be scheduled neatly into the day.

How this is done is the business of each house, just as it is the responsibility of each natural family. Some schedules need to be tighter than others, however. This depends on the needs of the children. It is part of the art of child care to determine these needs and how best to respond to them.

Weekly schedules are also determined by things outside of the family such as the weekly work or school schedule, church attendance, etc.

Weekly schedules can be fun and can be determined with the participation of all the family members. Weekly schedules can emphasize recreation or activities to occur on certain days of the week.

All scheduling should be preset and posted so all are aware of what happens next. The security we are after is based upon knowing what to expect.

Security and a sense of goal direction can be enhanced by the establishment of goals to be achieved by a certain date. An example of this would be: "If we can cut the light bill by $5.00

a month, we'll have a pizza party on May 14th." Or "On June 3rd, we'll clean house and then have a picnic."

The goal need not be a contingency. For example, "October 20th is Jim's birthday, we'll have a party; invite your best friend." Or, "We'll go the rollerderby on March 19th."

Such goals enhance the fun of group living. They further enhance the effects of security by their very irregularity. A promise made and followed through is an excellent model for the child to experience.

3. Consistency:

Scheduling implies consistency, but there are other ways that consistency can be used to enhance security.

One way is to do this through rules. Every group living situation requires rules to make it function smoothly.

Each rule should be specific, fair and enforceable. Rules should be as few as possible. A magilla of regulations is unenforceable and generally a joke.

Rules should also be reasonable. Rules which seem unreasonable are most often the occasion for rebellion.

Some rules are negotiable and some are not. "The wisdom to know the difference" is essential here. It does not hurt to have a family meeting every now and then to review old rules and establish new ones.

Non-negotiable rules include mandatory things such as curfew, licensing and policy standards, laws, and house rules related to cleanliness, respect for basic rights and treatment demands.

Negotiable rules include rules about use of television, phone calls, etc. Each house will find problems for which a rule will need to be negotiated as a solution. When a new rule is established, it needs a period of testing before it is reviewed. At least a week trial period is required, and possibly a month. All negotiable rules are subject to review.

When the group meets to discuss rules, they are learning the democratic process. Staff must realize the importance of the process for learning and not be too quick to jump in and solve problems. That would kill the process and thus, negate the learning process.

Chore assignments can be looked upon as a type of rule establishment. Doing chores has long been viewed as a way to teach responsibility. There is no reason to believe it is not.

That chores should be done is not negotiable. How and when they are done may be negotiable in some cases. Staff should participate in chores as well. The modeling influence of staff participation not only will instruct children in the correct way to do a particular chore, but will also teach by example that chore responsibilities do not cease at adulthood.

Doing chores help the child invest in the house. The child who just waxed the floor will not likely want anyone to leave a trail of mud across it.

When a time of day is established for each chore, it should be adhered to and not easily changed. While it is more important that the chore gets done than when it gets done in the average home, we are talking about the value of consistency. In the therapeutic milieu, structure and consistency are more important than the chore.

This should not be construed to mean that doing a chore well is not important. We are speaking here of the value of consistency and its _relative_ importance in the Therapeutic Group Home.

Rotating chores weekly is a good idea. It gives everyone a chance to experience a variety of duties within a consistent framework.

Another idea which you may find helpful in work assignments is to have a reinforcing group activity following upon the completion of each chore. After the rooms are swept in the afternoon, for example, dinner will be served. After the dinner dishes are done, we will sit down for a cup of coffee and a cigarette. The list is limited only by your imagination.

4. The New Kid:

A good part of consistency is the expectation of things which will be confirmed. To be therapeutic, you teach the child that what you say happens. This applies to each new child who enters the home.

The new child may be frightened and homesick as he enters this strange new world which is at least partially not of his/her own choosing. Besides an enthusiastic welcome, the child should be carefully and completely introduced to the new environment.

First, introduce yourself, then introduce each of the children who resides there. Show him/her the physical environment, where his/her room is, the bathroom, etc. (Some really topnotch staff make "Welcome _____" signs and arrange a feast in the new kid's honor.)

Very early, it is a good idea to sit down and discuss the whole routine with the child. If possible, have one of the residents sit down with you and the new child and let him or her explain the way things work.

The new child should also know that you care about him or her and that you also will be prepared to apply consequences for inappropriate behavior. Do not dwell on the negative, but do take time to explain that staff are not afraid to confront a child for the benefit of the child and that is an important part of caring.

Amidst all of this structure, consistency, and consequences, do not forget concern. During this stage of setting down expectations, let the child know that it is the staff's commitment to have concern for each child in the program.

The child must understand that when the agency takes a child in, the agency will not let go until it is in the best interests of the child to do so.

It is helpful in every case to explain the staff's commitment to children. As the child sees everything else being consistent, this commitment will be believed, too; and if this commitment is believed, it will not need to be tested very hard.

Sometime or other, a child will throw it in your face: "You just do this for pay; you don't really care!" How do you answer that? First of all, you don't. The charge is merely an attempt to get a reaction from you.

Secondarily, you do work for money, but you were hired because you are concerned for kids. Besides, nobody could pay you enough to make you concerned.

So when you respond, don't take it personally and do not make an argument out of what is really the equivalent of questioning your parental origins.

The child will not just accept your concern. He or she will test it. But, as stated above, this is more likely to be accepted when everything else is consistent. The new kid will finally have faith in your concern when it has been demonstrated over and over again.

In practice, concern is shown when you do not give up. But it is also shown when you are really interested in the child's interests, problems, accomplishments and failures. It is shown when you are worried about him or her and when you do something beyond the call of duty. All of this shows concern, but it will not be real until you have shown that you will remain consistent.

5. Variety:

An important component of consistency is the ability to inject some variety into it. The occasional surprise makes the routine fun.

Cold cereal may be the order of the day's routine for Tuesday breakfast. After this routine is well established, you may come in early and cook bacon and eggs. Think of how you would feel to have this special treat.

Plan a special event occasionally (especially in winter) that will break the routine. Sit down in your family meeting and say, "Things are getting dull. Let's do something this week which will break up this dull routine." You can then open up for suggestions, but be sure to have some ideas of your own.

Spontaneity is called for at times. Because it is spontaneity, it is difficult to prescribe. Inject the unplanned into the planned events. Here are some examples:

"Hey, there's a really interesting late movie on T.V. How would you like to stay up and watch it?"

"Hey, Joe, you've always wanted to work on cars. Want to help me hook up my new tape deck this afternoon?"

"It's too hot to eat in the dining room, let's go out and eat on the porch!"

A schedule should not be so rigid that individual needs cannot be considered. Circumstances and individuals sometimes require that we alter plans.

"Marice has a history exam tomorrow, so we should let her stay up an extra half hour to study."

"Matt has to work tonight, so he will eat later when he gets home."

Family living produces healthy members when there is a basic structure and a consistent, caring environment. Variety plays its

part in making life interesting and fun. Child care has before
it the challenge of producing consistency where chaos has produced
maladjustment. Through programming the environment, the living
situation, itself, becomes the greatest therapy available.

CHAPTER 5

HOW TO GET BURNT-OUT AND LOVE IT

"The kids are drivin' me crazy' I'm overworked, have had little sleep. I need a vacation, but there's no one to fill in when I'm gone. I can't last much longer'" After saying this, she went back to work, looking a bit frazzled.

A child care worker can't be expected to stand it very long-- or so some say. There are great demands placed on them, they have to be mother, father, counselor, chaplain, punching bag, maid, janitor, police and who knows what all. No doubt about it, you have chosen a very demanding job.

The lady quoted above is my mother. I was one of three who was driving her crazy. I bet you thought I was quoting a child care worker. It could have been. I just wanted to point out that child care workers act as "professional parents" and should not forget parents--mothers in particular--are also subject to unremitting pressures. They don't usually burn out, because no one gives them permission.

But child care workers do "burn out." They roll over and float belly up on the surface, signalling that a new one should be dropped into the tank. Occasionally, they flutter with a new spasm of life and thrash about for a while longer before the final stillness.

(There's some who believe that they see one of the belly uppers wink when no one is supposed to be looking. There is evidence to believe that they aren't really dead: They just taught each other the joys of floating in that posture.)

1. The "Burnt Out" Phenomenon:

When you came to work in child care, you met one or two "old pros" who probably have that relaxed manner which is at the same time fatigued and confident, knowing and yet pained. These "old pros" have probably clocked one or two--at the outside--three years. Of course, those years were packed with painful learning experiences.

Soon after you entered child care, the "old pro" quit. "Burnt out," he or she said. "Burnt out," the supervisor said, shaking his/her head. "Burnt out," you said to yourself, and you knew, deep in your heart, that you, too, will "burn out" someday.

And you will "burn out," unfortunately, unless you quit before you qualify as an "old pro." You will "burn out" because you are being taught to do so. It is expected by your supervisor, your co-workers, your mother, your boy or girlfriend, spouse and yourself. Too much depends on your eventual "burn out" for it not to happen. You owe it to tradition.

There will come a day when child care workers won't "burn out." No one will expect it to happen, so it won't. Child care workers will be respected, will work reasonable hours and will be compensated for their skills and their accomplishments. It will be a career. Am I dreaming? No, this is already happening.

Until this revolution reaches all of the far out boonies, we have to deal with the here and now.

Where did "burning out" start? It has an interesting history.

During World War II, two interesting and related developments occurred. One was the general acceptance of psychiatry and clinical psychology, and the other was the "Old Sergeant's Syndrome." They tie together.

It happened that some veteran soldiers who were on the line too long got really "spacey." They didn't sleep, didn't take care of their hygiene, lost all interests, and didn't really care about human life.

A few of these "old sergeants" were sent back to the "psycho wards" and they were analyzed and pampered. In a short time, an interesting contagion occurred: other soldiers got "battle fatigue" as it was called. At first, it was only the front liners, but it didn't take long before the clerical workers, who processed the paperwork for these cases, began to come down with it. Then orderlies got it, etc. etc.

The point is this: Any phenomenon which lets you fail with dignity is extremely coercive. You may not be able to resist it.

Speaking of failure, have you ever heard the one about "the mouse in the milk can?" The story goes that a mouse fell into a milk can, "plop!" There happened to be a man with a stopwatch standing there. He timed the mouse as he swam in the milk.

After a long time, the mouse was exhausted and reluctantly began to slip beneath the surface. The man rescued it and put it in a box for a week or two of recuperation.

After he was certain that the mouse had thoroughly regained its strength, he dropped it back into a similar milk can. It swam half as long as before, then gave up. He rescued it again, let it recuperate again and then found that the mouse swam only about one fourth of the original time.

There have been no comparative studies to show which is a more difficult situation, the milk can for the mouse, or child care for the child care worker. But the analogy tells us that the more we are rescued, the more we will tend to give up before we have to.

Do mice get "burnt out" in milk cans like child care workers do in their work? On the surface, it looks like a very similar situation. It points out that you can indeed get exhausted when your strength is gone. So, failure can be a natural thing. On the other hand, the real feeling of exhaustion can occur before we reach our physical (and emotional) limits. We can, and do, get conditioned to fail too soon.

The "burn out" is real, and it is not real. It is real in that the conditioning that occurs is real, the feelings are real, and the fact of giving up is real. It is unreal in that it need not happen. Different conditioning could lead to hanging in there longer and better.

2. How It Works:

People (and mice) give up, quit, fail, "burn out" and drop out because there is insufficient pay off or reward for continuing combined with too much punishment and enough support for giving up. It is like that in anything we do. These factors are arranged for us or by us, and, depending upon our past experiences in milk cans, we are going to keep drowning earlier and earlier or keep swimming.

All of this analogy is merely to vividly demonstrate how the "burnt out" phenomenon works. The ingredients are: 1) Little pay off; 2) punishment; 3) reinforcement for the emotional by-products from the first two. Let's see how it works in child care.

First of all, you get little pay off for maximum effort. Day after day, week after week, you put out your best efforts and intentions for the kids. You really spend your guts and what happens? Freddy Fastfingers steals your car and plows into the back of a truck. When he gets back to the house, he laughs his head off as you try to explain to an irate trucker about emotionally disturbed kids and how you really do supervise them, but you have to go to the bathroom sometimes.

It may not be so dramatic, but let's face it, the kids will give you little immediate pay off for your efforts. When you realize that you may begin to think of yourself as a martyr, doing an impossible job for kids who need you, and yet no "thank you's" are forthcoming. So, you might just as well hang it up.

It isn't just the kids. Your mother is anxiously awaiting the time when you quit messing around and get a real job. The people at the bank also look at you funny when you tell them you're in child care when you try to borrow money to get your car fixed. You might as well be a seal hunter in the Sahara.

A few people might admire you for your work, but darned few. And you, yourself, are absolutely certain you could be doing something else with a little more status attached. Let's face it, child care worker appreciation doesn't rank as high in the socio-economic scheme of things as it should. As things stand now, you aren't going to get all the strokes you do deserve.

A word about money. Money, in the form of salary, is not enough of a reinforcer to keep you working at any job. You might do a lot to keep from losing it, but you are working minute by minute because the job you are doing means something to you. While you deserve an adequate salary, you will not work harder for more money. You will work for other strokes, folks.

Punishment often comes from supervisors. You are out there, busting your buns and nobody seems to notice or care. Well, that's not too bad. But one day you take your eyes off Millie Moppet and she jabs out Portly Portnoy's left eye and you get hell. Or you forget to give Effie Peptick her six o'clock pill and she convulses into a pot of boiling beans. Your job is now on the line and everyone thinks you're about the lowest scum since the inventor of pay toilets.

Reinforcement which leads to "burnt out" comes from your peers. If you have accepted the martyr role, you find many people who will agree with you because they are in the same boat. It is well known that emotionally pained people find "comfort" together and child care workers are no exception. Seeking comfort can lead to reinforcing martyrdom.

Make no mistake about it, misery loves company and such company makes misery. It works so subtly that you don't even notice, and the resulting debilitation is real. Rashes and ulcers are prominent among the physical reactions to emotional states. Your energy level is also dependent upon how you are doing emotionally. If you are being maintained in an emotionally depressed state, you are what we call "burnt out."

The mechanism involved is the reinforcement process. You are occasionally reinforced (given sympathy, attention, a hug or what have you) for your depressed state. In time, the strength of intermittent reinforcement takes hold of you and the state becomes stronger, more frequent and more pervasive.

It finally can reach a point where quitting is the only option for you. You will find you are losing friends, not working well, drinking too much, smoking too much, not sleeping well, forgetting your mother on Mother's Day, and that your plants die when you talk to them. Quit before this point, if possible, and before you hurt somebody.

3. Expectations:

"Tell me somthing," Darryl said, "Did you just happen to end up here or did you always wanna take care of crazy kids when you grew up?"

Darryl had a way with words. He'd been in child care for five years, from the kid's side of the keys. He'd seen a lot of people come and go and I guess you could say he ran the best training program around, with the help of a few of his contemporaries. His question stuck with me because it made me think.

No, Darryl, I didn't always want to be in child care when I grew up. Tell me something, who did? We all wanted to do different things. Cowboy, fireman, physician, teacher, dentist, nurse, pilot, international jewel thief, psychologist, urban planner, trucker—all of these or more have been in our minds from time to time as we plotted our careers. It's the rare bird among us who actually planned to be a child care worker four years ago.

"Burning out" is equally related to the prestige of a position. If you were taught to look upon a profession as worthwhile, you are likely to feel it is important. Folklore about certain jobs can make them or break them. What is the folklore of child care; what are its traditional roots?

First of all, child care started, in the main, with "house mothers" who took in curly headed (white) orphans and turned them into bank presidents and ballplayers. Later on, "houseparents" came along when a retired couple was hired to do the job. They live in, had a garden around the cottage, baked cookies and made kites that flew.

Later on, the orphans went to foster homes and the window breaking, foul mouthed, cigarette smoking, car thieves who hate baths took their place. The house mothers headed for the safety of their dreams and Social Security and the houseparents were now college dropouts who needed work. The prominence of psychology and psychiatric treatment turned the kids into "emotionally disturbed" and the houseparents into child care staff and their education and training became imperative.

This history covers thirty or forty years, a relatively short period. The evolution of vocations makes it pretty certain that the next ten years will see child care recognized as a valid and important vocation. Already, college courses in child care exist, some workers are unionized, and the salary range is showing encouraging growth even now. With this evolution, we should see the position recognized and the link with the soft mother broken, and the "burn out" will be a rarity.

The first "burn out" is probably still alive and well, selling Fords in Bloomington. Those who learned to be "burnt out" after him or her are only a few years away from you, and their followers just left child care a year or so ago. The tradition isn't too old. It can be corrected and put in perspective.

As long as child care is seen as an unimportant vocation that only the bleeding heart and the otherwise unemployable gravitate toward, then it will not have people in it who will resist "burning out." The kids will not be served by the constant parade of "burnt out" martyrs stamping each child with "Failure" as they pass on to their "real careers."

Other vocations are demanding, but only a rare instance finds someone becoming a basket case. Almost every kind of medical profession is a real pressure cooker from training to retirement. Sure, some do drop out, but society doesn't expect these people to "burn out," so they don't fizzle as easily. The public image of this professional is success, competence and objectivity, not martyrdom.

41

Peer influence is extremely important to all of us. It, more than society, may influence you. When you get into child care, you may find that your friends treat you differently. Why? Because you are different.

Think about it. You are now intimately involved in the most important job in your life. You aren't just in child care, like you would be in accounting or fast food franchises. You are up to your heart in a few individuals and up to your eye balls in a lot of stuff you're learning about the extremes of human nature, yours and theirs.

You make boring company after a while. You are obsessed with children and with tiny successes and molehills you call mountains. You get turned on by some new muscles you find yourself flexing in your head and some hot and cold feelings that you never felt before. Don't be surprised that you find people yawning or at least not understanding what you are talking about.

Peers in child care are your best friends and your deadliest enemies. As stated and implied before, they are the perpetuators of the folklore of "burn out." There is the danger of too much mental inbreeding in any job when birds of a feather start congregating on the same park statue.

Another danger is the salary trap. Child care salaries are not so huge that you are apt to get stuck in the field because it pays so much that you can't move on. But in a tight economy, you might be tempted to strain yourself to hold onto the security of any job.

Don't. You can't do it, and it helps no one for you to try to fake it.

But while you are trying to find out whether you want this job, live cheaply and ferret away some nuts and berries for the winter.

We all need to avoid getting into a position where we can't afford to quit. It's a losing game because your supervisor will not let you hurt the kids to save your car payments.

4. How To Maintain Your Sanity:

The Fiddler is trying to pick out a tune while balancing on the roof. Why is he up there? Tradition. How does he keep his balance? Tradition.

And there you are, like the Fiddler, in the same quandary. You work to maintain your sanity. Why do you have to work so hard at it? Because you're in child care. So why are you in child care? The answer is that you are doing so because it's you.

Like the Fiddler, in that ridiculous position, you strive to maintain your balance. And how do you do that? Balance.

Balance what you are responsible for versus what others are responsible for. Know your job description and know that there are a lot of other people involved. Everything doesn't lie on your head.

Balance your life. Get plenty of healthy experiences. Don't let your job take any big bites out of your private life. Don't sacrifice your butterfly collection, friends, and Presley records for the job. It's a dumb sacrifice anyhow, because you will not last longer by selling all that you are for any job.

Balance your eating habits. A sickly child care worker is no use to anyone. Eat well.

Balance your work day. Try to sit down occasionally, or try to interject some fun into those horrible days while treasuring those happy moments that do come along.

Get the idea? Don't drown in the job. Give all you've got, but put some back as soon as you can.

Recognize your "downs." Everybody gets depressed every now and then. Those biorhythm nuts are beginning to make sense when they say that moods come and go regularly. So when you're down, don't be too quick to blame your incompetence or the job. Deal with it.

Admit it. Tell yourself, "Hey, I'm really feeling low today!" Then promise yourself you will try not to spread it around.

Get busy. Don't give yourself time to try to brood over your depression. This type of rumination is extremely unproductive. Worry doesn't go away if you worry about it.

Arrange some excitement in your life. Change your personal schedules around to break the monotony. Call your best friend or build a bookshelf. Action is the best cure.

If you do have a problem to worry about, be realistic. Don't drag it around in your head like a dead fish, smelling up your life. Get it out and take action. Talk to your best friend about it.

If you're lying awake worrying, try this. Imagine the worst possible outcome, then decide what you'll do in that event. Now, you've proven the problem can be solved. They aren't going to kill you, whoever they are. And if they do, you haunt 'em.

Avoid the sympathetic. They are going to rub your nose in your problems, magnify your weaknesses, and they won't pay for your ulcer. After they've ruined you, they'll move on to someone else. They're good hearted souls; they mean well, but don't let them hurt you.

When you find someone jumping in with all that sympathy, stop and change the subject. Or say, "Hey, this is ridiculous! I'm a big boy (girl) now and I'm too old to be coddled."

Above all, keep your thoughts about the job and yourself healthy. You're ok, and the job is extremely important. No one can do it quite like you can and you're getting better at it.

Finally, don't count on the kids. They aren't going to perk you up. It isn't their job. They don't need to know your problems. (Say it three times: They are the kids, I am the staff.)

Count on them not to make life easy when you need to have life easy. On the contrary, they are going to teach you that you can stretch your endurance and patience beyond what you ever thought possible.

One time you will get an extra charge from the kids, maybe twice, maybe more. But you should never ever let yourself get into the habit of expecting it.

If this job is ever going to get the dignity it deserves, it will come, in part, because you make it so. Make the effort to convince yourself that you are in one of the youngest and certainly the most important vocations in the world. Be a pioneer, not a martyr.

5. How To Quit:

The citizens of Catatonia were not noted for their mental dexterity. However, they had a great deal of pride and resented anyone challenging their pride or virtue in any way.

One day, an Irishman stood on the plateau above the town. He cupped his hands to his mouth and said, "Catatonians are dumb slobs. I can lick any one of ye."

Well, the Catatonians sent their head knocking champion up the hill and waited.

Two hours later, they heard the Irishman again, "Is that the best you have to offer! I'm one lone Irishman and I can whip any two of you!"

Up went two burley Catatonians. But two hours later, the Irishman taunted them again.

"Ye'd better send a gang. It looks like one lone Irishman is too much for ye!"

Catatonians hate to look foolish in front of anyone, even a lone Irishman. They realized they had to shut him up, so they sent up their local militia, forty-three men with clubs and pitchforks. The townsfolk listened to the groanings and thuds through the night.

Sunrise found the Irishman appearing again, holding the tattered banner of the militia. "So much for yer knitting circle! I, one lone Irishman, have proven to the world that Catatonians are clods and fools."

By this time, the word reached the capitol of Catatonia, and the army was sent out. The people cheered as the Royal Army of Catatonia marched through the streets. Women wept and old men felt a lump in the throat as the brown and purple banner was proudly borne down the street and up the hill to put an end to the Irishman and his taunting jibes.

For three days, two hundred of Catatonia's best were heard clashing in mortal combat. Clouds of dust were seen rising above the crest of the plateau. Finally, by noon of the fourth day, all was silent.

A peace delegation was sent immediately, waving white banners. They reached the plateau and the sight was terrible. Broken bodies, scattered about, blood and gore were everywhere. From under a pile of rubble a hand was seen to move, beckoning the horrified delegation to come over.

As they came close, they noticed the poor twisted body of the soldier who summoned them to draw still nearer. They bent down to hear what he would say, "The Irishman . . . he lied; there were two of them!"

The Catatonians apparently didn't know when to quit. . . . Do you?

Child care is like alcohol. As long as you are enjoying it and can use it in the right balance with everything else in your life, it is fine. But once it controls you, when you find all of your values in life are crumbling because of it, when you find it hanging on and sucking the blood out of your life--quit.

When you start, you will go through a period of time when the job seems to be possessing you. That is a natural phenomenon. Any challenging job will affect you that way. But if it gets to the point where over a period of weeks, you are being run by the job, then you'd better check your marbles to see if any are missing.

Ask yourself some serious questions. Are you into child care to feel like you feel most of the time? Do you understand that you don't have to stay? Do you know when you are going to quit? Are you sacrificing too much for this job?

I once had a very serious career man, of the Alamedo Dairy in Omaha, set me down and gently break the news to me that I might not have what it takes to be an Alamedo man. Bent, crushed and broken, I wondered if I would have to resort to some lesser professional like Supreme Court Justice or neurosurgeon.

Well, pal, you may be faced with the same predicament. Child care work, like Alamedo Dairy work, just isn't for everyone. It is no shame to face this fact and leave.

First, seek a conference with your supervisor before you make your final decision. The supervisor has seen many people come and go and will have the objectivity to help you decide. If you want to stay and are having a hard time of it, let him or her know.

Next, give yourself time, two weeks or more before you make your decision. During that time, try to use suggestions from your supervisor or peers to make it work. Also, examine your moods and intentions.

Finally, if you decide to quit, give notice in writing. Your personnel record will record that you were a good employee and quit in an acceptable manner.

Tell the kids. Tell them honestly that you didn't have what it takes and they deserve the best and you couldn't give it. Keep giving them this message no matter how much they act up.

Finally, make sure you have received some sort of termination interview. This will tell you if you will get a recommendation from the agency when you leave.

Remember what Shakespeare wrote in Hamlet:

"First of all, unto thine own self be true and all else will follow as the day the night." That is true in life and true in child care in a very concentrated way. Never ever hang on for any other reason than that you are getting some kind of fulfillment from the work. And after you've tried it and find you don't like it, and can't do it, don't hang around.

Like the autistic kid said when the psychiatrist asked why he beat his head against the wall:

"It feels so good when I quit'"

CHAPTER 6

FACING PROBLEMS
(The O.K. Corral, Take 1,001)

If there is anything that wears you out in caring for children, it is the constant press of problems in an atmosphere where you are drained by the needs of children. Not that you aren't sometimes rejuvenated in your work, but it is a rare day when you don't have to fight off the urge to wrestle problems through the night.

You don't have much choice but to face problems in this business. You cannot put them all off. Sometimes they are standing in front of you screaming in your face. How you handle them may well determine whether they get better or get worse. In another sense, your handling of problems determines how long and how well you endure.

This chapter offers some suggestions and approaches to problems and problem situations. It helps you in defining and analyzing problems, seeking solutions and handling confrontations.

1. Defining Problems:

The first step in finding solutions is asking the right questions and defining the problems. It isn't uncommon at all to feel there is something wrong and not quite know what. The urge to go off half-cocked seeking the cure without really understanding the disease is extremely common.

In child care, you will constantly find yourself rushing in with a solution before you understand the problem, only to find your solution has become a problem. There is no way you can totally become immune to this because things often happen too quickly. You can't always sit down and map things out ahead of time. And (Be honest!) sometimes in a fit of impatience, you almost deliberately choose the wrong thing, say the hurtful thing, take the more selfish course of action.

Child care is a trying business, sometimes more like war than love, and all of those angelic intentions we have (or had) melt away in the rattling of the spears and shields of daily living. But in our saner moments, we can reflect and correct, and gradually we can decrease the errors and increase the correct courses of action. In this chapter, you will become acquainted with some options in thinking about problems.

Let's look at attitudes toward problems. The first thing to keep in mind is that your approach to any problem should be a positive one. We are in the business where a foolhardy "it-can-be-done" attitude is absolutely essential. No problem is soluble if the solvers believe it is insoluble.

After we have decided that the problem has to have a solution, we must believe we can find it. Often we are hampered by believing we have to have an expert give us the answer. While we may use the expert, he or she will not be of use to us until we have thought out the problem a little more.

The third element of attitude we need is the assurance that while we may not come up with the best or only answer, we will probably not be too far off and there is value in trying. This value lies in thinking through the problem.

After we have our attitudes straight, we can begin to define the problem. In order to do so, we should answer a series of questions:

1. What makes us believe there is a problem?

2. What do we observe?

3. Under what conditions do we observe these things?

4. Is there a pattern indicating a commonality, or are there several separate problems?

5. Who owns the problem(s) and why?

6. In terms of the total picture, what priority does this problem have?

The above questions help us come up with a statement of the problem. They help us decide if it really is a problem, or whether it is a personality clash. When we have answered the above, we can make a problem statement and start working toward a hypothesis for its solution.

What sort of problems are we talking about? Any at all. They could be anything from a leaky roof to a broken heart. Let's look at a sample situation and test out the questions.

The child in this case is a seventeen year old high school student. He has been in many placements and had "blown" all of them until he came to the agency in question, where he was placed in a group home. There he began to repeat his previous behavior patterns and was in danger of having the rejection pattern renewed.

Marty's behavior was obnoxious. He had honed the ability to irritate others to a fine cutting edge. The staff's reaction was divided. It was obvious that Marty related adequately at school, at his part-time job and with a few friends.

The first question in defining the problem brought a mixed response. What made us think there was a problem was that all staff wanted to kill him and the other kids were also upset.

What do we observe? We observe that he resents authority and, with high frequency, he verbally attacks the person in authority.

Under what circumstances? This seems to occur only when child care authority is asserted. He seems to handle other situations, if not perfectly, at least better. This also answered the next questions about commonality.

Ownership of the problem elicited a mixed answer. On the one hand, it was obvious that Marty had this problem over many placements. On the other hand, it was obviously situational. It was a problem found only in Marty and not in the other kids, and many approaches have been experimented with in the house to no avail. Thus, we rejected the staff's ownership of the problem.

The consensus was that the problem was mainly situational. One dissention was that Marty's authority problem may have repercussions when he is a parent. However, this opinion was not adequately supported.

Finally, the priority angle was approached. Those who wanted to confront Marty on the problem decided at this point that other solutions needed to be found. After all, he had roughly another year left before he would be on his own. The chance of treating the problem effectively was risky, and no one could be sure that it could be done in that time. Furthermore, the situational nature of the problem made the long term effects of such a strategy seem somewhat dubious.

The problem was stated thus: Marty has a situational reaction to staff authority which hampers his growth in placement.

(An apartment with a roommate-advocate proved to be a more congenial arrangement.)

2. Brain Storming:

Moving on, let us assume that we have defined a problem. It is right there in front of us, sticking out like a purple thumb. Now what do we do?

One solution used in some places has been called "brainstorming." You know it from those cliche jokes about "running it up the flagpole to see who salutes it" and all of that. Well, that's what we are talking about, but it isn't exactly like that.

The object of brainstorming is to get as many ideas out as possible. From that process we hope to have many possible solutions. Certain conditions have to be met to make the ideas flow:

1. You have to be free from outside interruptions.

2. Have several people present.

3. It is helpful to have a more peripheral person or two. That way the group can overcome its tendency to think alike.

4. Nobody is "the guru."

5. Write down every idea.

6. No idea is rejected.

Brainstorming sessions are exercises in imagination. Because our imaginations are often too controlled, it is absolutely essential that no idea be rejected. In fact, it is sometimes beneficial to throw out some obviously impractical ideas. These ideas often generate more practical ideas. One session serves as an example.

The boy in question had been verbally assaulting female staff. To start the sessions, a ridiculous idea was put forth which led to some more practical solutions.

1. "We could cut his tongue out."

2. "Or tie his mouth shut."

3. "Have him keep silent as a consequence."

4. "Reinforce his controlling his comments."

5. "Have him repeat comments with apologies."

etc.

51

Brainstorming sessions should yield a large list of ideas which the group reviews when ideas have stopped. The object at this part of the session is to still remain open while being critical. If an idea is impractical, how could it be made practical? Is there a principle involved which can be applied in a more practical manner?

3. Outcome Analysis:

In any conflict situation, the possible outcomes will be somewhere along a continuum from win to lose. Conflicts are more like negotiation than competitive sports in that the ultimate winning situation is one in which everyone wins and the conflicts are resolved with the least harm done.

(At the same time, we must remember that in the field of child care, some learning may be inherent in conflicts resolution. The child can learn how to handle feelings and how to resolve the conflict humanely.)

Outcome analysis is what it sounds like. Whenever you consider a possible response to a problem, you must think ahead to the probable outcomes. If the probable results of your contemplated actions are negative, then it is best to look for another response.

Again, an example can make these abstractions clear:

Ed has abused his privilege of staying out until midnight. Because he has done this before, the staff have decided to restrict him to the house for four weeks. In Ed's particular case, was this the best solution.

Knowing Ed, the supervisor decides to reduce the restriction. Why? Ed has a habit of running away when he is restricted, and so it is resolved that in view of Ed's probation status, it would be best not to paint Ed into that particular corner.

In another situation, risk taking is more evident. Three twelve year olds had climbed part way up a water tower. Others cheered them on. The adults were unable to coax them down and in defiance, the youngsters pleased their audience by ascending even higher.

The outcome analysis led to a risk but an unavoidable one. The adults ignored the climbers and moved the audience out of sight. In less than ten minutes the adventurers were safely down under their own power.

The analysis was quite obvious: To pursue the kids meant they would perform and take more risks. To remove the audience meant taking a chance, but, in terms of the dynamics involved and outcomes probable, it seemed to be the best response.

It is obvious that conflict and crisis situations involve different stakes for us from what they do for the kids. The kids' goals are more immediate and definitely are highly bound to self interest. Ours, presumably, are more aimed at helping the child (hopefully). Pay explicit attention to this fact! If you do not recognize the fact that there are two games being played, there will be only one—the child's!

4. Communication:

It isn't unusual that a lot of packaged therapy programs emphasize communication. Some of these programs instruct parents how to be "effective," others how to give "strokes," and on it goes. It seems like someone is always playing with ways to communicate (i.e. how to manipulate with words).

They are correct. Communication is central to human existence. It is so strong an influence in our lives that we judge people in terms of it. We say that a person is "difficult to get through to," we "can't _relate_ to him/her (or even it)." We have other communication labels in our vocabularies like "I can't _tell_ the difference." and "I would _say_ so." All of these communication phrases are symbols for other concepts, but they give us some idea of how important communication is (in case you didn't know).

Listening is hearing on purpose. It is also hearing what is being communicated, not just what is said. Our words are instruments for communicating. It's like a code, a set of culturally defined symbols that identify simple and complex concepts which are more or less the same to the sender and receiver.

The message, "I am angry," may come out in a lot of ways. For instance, the words may be, "Get your damn butt off the furniture!" or it may be the slamming of a door. As a rule, people don't become more reasonable as they become more upset.

The task of the child care worker is to remain objective. Thus, when the child calls you a "m/fing. S.O.B.," you don't respond in kind, you respond in a way that will demonstrate for the child a model of rational response. First of all, you don't trade pain for pain. You stop that self-defeating spiral by remaining calm and finding out what the problem is. Often it may have little to do with you, but you won't know until you have found out.

How do you find out? You can ask. Sometimes that works if you do it right. But sometimes it only makes things worse.

The other thing you can do is try some reflective responses:

Kid: "You g-d-mf, why don't you go to hell!"

You: "You're really angry at me."

Kid: "You're damn right!"

You: "I wish I knew what's bugging you."

Kid: "You're just like those damn teachers, you never listen to my side."

You: "Teachers seem unfair at times?"

Kid: "Yeah!"

You: "Did you get hassled today?"

Kid: "Mr. Baker, that c/s, gave me a detention for talking back to him. I've talked back before and he never said shit!"

You: "I guess that really bugs you. I'd probably feel the same!"

Kid: "Yeah, but everything seems like that sometimes."

This conversation could probably go on and on until the kid got the problem off his/her chest (that solves one problem) and perhaps, you might even come up with a solution. In any event, you have communicated that you care and you will listen and that may be the best communication of all.

It is important, no matter how you communicate, that you are aware that you are teaching, generally through modeling, how to communicate. If you scream, they will scream. If you swear, they will swear, and if you analyze the problem (out loud), they will learn how to do that.

It isn't possible to overemphasize the modeling effects of the adult in the child's world. You have some influence and probably a great one. If you squelch communication, the child will not learn to listen to others. In communication, you are the message.

54

5. Commands:

Someone is always giving orders. Some people have to be more diplomatic than others. The drill sergeant's "TEN HUP'" is much more brusk than his request to "Please pass the potatoes" while eating with the captain and his wife.

The style of a command or order is, or should be, consistent with the relationship and the purpose of the communication. For instance, you can get away with shouting "Look out!", but to use the same tone of voice to get someone to move over so you can sit on the couch might produce bruises and lacerations.

This may make sense, but it is very often violated in relating to children. Adult attitudes seem to be that the child is a lower form of animal and that we are higher. They can do no right, we can do no wrong. They must respect adults, we don't have to respect them.

You can see where this is leading. We must learn to respect the feelings and worth of the individual when we talk to anyone, and this includes children.

Some linguist came up with a definition of "respect" which makes sense here. Respect means look at (spect) again or intensively (re). An example might be the carpenter who respects the wood and, therefore, can build with it. Without respect, he would be working against the grain and the beautiful cabinet would never be a reality.

So, if you respect the child, you will work with the grain and not against it when giving commands.

For one thing, you don't give a command when you don't need to do so. You also don't command what you can't expect. Your respect will dictate when a simple request is sufficient.

1. "Please don't put your feet on the coffee table."

2. "Get your filthy clod hoppers off the coffee table!"

3. "When I was your age, I knew better than to put my feet on the furniture."

4. "How many times have I told you not to put your feet on the coffee table?"

5. "Good children respect furniture."

How would an adolescent respond to each of these statements? How would you respond to them? Why should there be a difference?

Clarity is often missed in communication. You not only have to know what to say, but you have to say it clearly enough so that the other person understands the meaning, too. Otherwise, you aren't communicating.

Be clear in what effect you want. Mother screamed at Jimmy: "Quit pulling the cat's tail!" (The cat kept on screeching painfully.) "Jimmy, didn't I tell you to quit pulling the cat's tail?" "Yes, Mother, and I did. Now he's pulling it, I'm just hanging on."

Probably Jimmy understood, but since he intended to be a lawyer someday, he demanded greater clarity. Mother, already holding position as judge and executioner, quickly rendered judgment and rapid execution.

Some commands are clearer than others. "Behave yourself" is pretty broad. Some of us will know what that means, but in many cases, you have to be more explicit: "You have permission to go to the movie at Cinema II, have something to eat afterwards and be home by 12:30."

It isn't that you have to spell out every detail and agonize over it like a legal document. A certain amount of sense is presumed on the part of the child when you communicate. But don't blame the child if his/her honest opinion of what you said and meant is incorrect by your frame of reference.

To achieve clarity, be sure you set times, conditions, performance and criteria as they pertain to the command.

"Your job is to empty the garbage, which includes emptying all the waste paper baskets into a garbage bag, picking up all papers and other throw-aways and putting all trash in bags in the garage. This is to be done each evening before 7:00 p.m."

Now, that is pretty clear. It could be simplified by saying: "Put all garbage into bags and put them in the garage by 7:00 p.m. each day."

Other chore commands would emphasize criteria: "The table is considered clean when all visible crumbs, etc. are removed and no dried or wet spots remain."

Certain commands require an additional element: Contingency. We sometimes have to threaten and say, "You do _____, or else." or "You do that, and _____!" Many rules of conduct need to hold some contingency of that order, if we expect compliance. In establishing rules, or yourself as reliable, you need clear-cut contingencies for positive and negative events which will be consistently adhered to. These are usually contrived contingencies.

Other contingencies are natural contingencies. These flow naturally in a sensible way from the behavior. These contingencies often bring about compliance without an uproar. For example: "After you clear the table, we'll eat" or "When the car has been washed, we'll go to the lake."

Other commands have contingencies that are in between: "When you've settled down, we'll turn on the T.V.!" Another example is one a child care worker once used effectively. While Scott was driving the wagon along with eight kids, they became really noisy and it was getting on his nerves. He pulled over, stopped the car and said to the dismayed group, "When you're loud like that I can't concentrate on driving. If I can't concentrate on driving, I can't drive safely. So, I will wait here until you are ready to go on."

The effect was immediate. The children agreed to be quiet and did. Scott gave them a rationale for his consequence and while they grumbled, they agreed to it.

This brings us to another point. How much rationale does a child need? Some adults become really apologetic and nervous when they try to explain over and over again the reason for their rules or commands. That is a mistake, and it means that the child is manipulating you.

Everyone deserves some explanation most of the time, but once you have clearly explained the rationale, you are done arguing, explaining and apologizing. Even two year old toddlers can befuddle adults with "Why?" Adolescents get a little more sophisticated at arguing with the rules, but it's still the same delaying action.

Look at the kid's game plan. "I have been told to be home at 10:00. That's the rule. If I accept that, then I'm stuck with it. If I argue with it, it probably won't get any earlier, and I have a small chance it might be later. Ergo: I argue."

Kids are always thinking like that. That goes for me, too.

To sum up: 1. Respect the child as a person equal to you in rights and dignity. 2. Be clear in your rules and commands. 3. Use clear, enforceable contingencies which are natural, if possible.

6. Correcting:

They put erasers on pencils because people make mistakes. They do not put erasers on kids, so I guess it is up to us.

When correcting, it is important to remember the "golden rule." If you treat others as you would like to be treated, you probably won't create a problem while trying to correct one. Try the following when correcting:

The first thing to remember is to note the good that was done, if possible. Next, we objectively point out the error or misbehavior. Third, we explain the way it should be done, or offer some options. (We may even want to demonstrate.) Finally, we praise the correct performance or choice of alternatives.

Let's take a simple chore situation first. The scene is a group home. Georgia is cleaning the table. She quickly announces, "I'm done!"

(Praise)	Staff:	"I see you did a good job getting the dishes off and getting the crumbs off."
(Point out)		"But you missed some spots where the water stained the table and dried."
(Instruct)		"Let me show you. You really have to rub with a wet cloth to get them out."
(Performance)		"Now, you try it."
(Praise)		"Now, that looks much better. You've done it perfectly."

Let's now take a more complicated case; same scene, same players. This time, Georgia has come home at 1:00 a.m. She was expected at 10:30. In this case, we add something.

	Georgia:	"I'm sorry I'm late. My date's car broke down and . . ."
	Staff:	"Georgia, I'm really upset at this. I was worried. You should have called."
	Georgia:	"I'm sorry. . ."
(Praise)	Staff:	"I accept your apology. It is very adult of you to say you're sorry . . ."
(Point out)		"But you knew you should have called, and I'm not sure you're telling the truth about the car breaking down."
	Georgia:	"Am I restricted?

58

	Staff:	"Yes, you know the rule. You are restricted for a week."
	Georgia:	"Oh, Damn!"
(Options)	Staff:	"What could you have done to avoid this restriction?"
	Georgia:	"I could have called. I was at a party and had no way to get back. I didn't want to seem too goody-goody and 'call mommy'."
	Staff:	"How could you have saved your pride, kept your friends, and still made it in by 10:30?"
	Georgia:	"I don't know."
	Staff:	"Would it have helped if you told your date that you had to be home by 10:30 when you went out so he would know from the beginning?"
	Georgia:	"I did, I think."
	Staff:	"How can you get it across to him so he will know you mean it next time?"
(Viable option)	Georgia:	"Maybe, if you explained it to him the next time we go out and told him about restrictions."
(Praise)	Staff:	"That sounds like a good idea. I really think you've come up with a really good solution. That shows a lot of maturity."
	Georgia:	"Am I still on restriction?"
	Staff:	"Yep!"

No doubt, this example could be complicated in real life by having to deal with emotional issues. This a model of problem solving and correction which will minimize the multiplication of problems and provide a model for the child to use.

7. Confronting:

Kids aren't referred to us for their endearing qualities. Kids we see in child care have problems that must be dealt with. The question is: How do we deal with them? Furthermore, we need to align them with the priorities of the treatment goals and objectives.

One technique is called confronting. Confronting is the act of not letting the child be irresponsible or manipulative. It can be "soft" or "hard." Soft confronting is when you use non-arousal techniques like humor, listening, counseling, etc., to make the child face the situation. Hard confronting is when you are very direct and may face emotional and even physical reactions to the confrontation. (Little effective confronting can be done without a relationship, so don't start off day one!)

Al was very forlorn. He had just lost another girlfriend. This one lasted for two dates, which makes it almost a long term courtship in comparison to Al's previous experiences.

John had been Al's child care worker for nearly a year and had developed a pretty good relationship with him. John could see how depressed Al was at his lack of interpersonal skills.

"Al, I see how depressed you are. Wanna shoot some baskets?"

"Nah, I don't feel like it."

John throws the ball to Al, who catches it. "Come on, Al, just a couple of shots!"

To make a long story short, John gets Al to moving around, shooting baskets, creating positive atmosphere. Next, John shoots some confrontation (soft) and Al can deal with them:

"I think you come on too strong with the ladies, Al."

"I don't know what I'm doing wrong."

Rather than continuing with some dialogue here, suffice it to say that John pulled off a soft confrontation, individualized to meet Al's needs and temperament.

Hard confrontations involve emotional arousal and the possibility of physical acting out. Be darned sure you are ready to handle the effects of it before you get started.

Martha's money was gone. She had left her purse in the kitchen and when she came back for it, it was open and ten dollars were missing. Everyone was in the living room except Dan, who had been in the dining room next to the kitchen.

Martha: "Dan, ten dollars are missing from my purse."

Dan: "I didn't take it. I wasn't near it!"

Martha: "You were the only one who could have taken it."

Dan: "I'm getting out of here. No one's accusing me of stealing!"

Martha: (blocking the door) "You're not leaving!"

Now begins the screaming and swearing on Dan's part. Martha holds her own and insists on the money being returned. To make a long story short, Dan finally returns the money, but that isn't the end of it. The point of the confrontation was not just ten dollars, the point was honesty and trust. The hard confrontation leads to a softer one until (and it may take hours) Dan understands the importance of honesty and trust.

Confrontation can take a lot out of everyone. After awhile, you get tired of the hassles and may want to let it slide by. You can't do that. You have to make the kid feel the responsibility for his or her actions. If you quit confronting, you quit doing child care.

But you don't confront everything. We all have our safe little games to play, and we don't expect to be confronted on everything. You confront according to a treatment plan, with a goal in mind and means of evaluation. You confront for change.

A final point: As they say in Vaudeville, "Always leave 'em laughing!" Translated into child care, this means that you stay with the confrontation until a solution is found and everyone can go away feeling as good as possible.

The problem should be resolved with some action or proposed course of action. Sometimes it may be an apology, sometimes it is restitution of some sort. Whatever it is, there is an act that resolves it.

Finally, forget it. The confrontation is over when it is over. It is not dragged on for even a minute. There is no reason to continue to throw the problem up in the kid's face when he or she has resolved to perform the act that resolves it.

Remember: "Do unto others as you would have others do unto you." I guess that sums up what we have been talking about.

CHAPTER 7

NORMAL REACTIONS TO ABNORMAL SITUATIONS
(and Vice Versa)

Junior sat on the bench in the emergency room. He stared straight ahead. His nose was running and his eyes watered. When the doctor came out, he asked, "How old are you, Son?"

His sister answered, "He's eight, but he won't tell you 'cause he don't talk to no grownups."

For over two years, Junior hadn't spoken to adults, and that was connected to the many scars the doctor saw when he removed Junior's shirt. You see, Junior used to stutter until his daddy tried a very painful cure. After that, no adult ever heard Junior stutter again.

Marlene was in college now. She was a frightened young blonde of twenty one who seemed too nervous while the counselor talked to her. She wanted her schedule changed because she was flunking English. When it looked like the counselor was becoming sympathetic, she suddenly calmed down, unbuttoned two buttons on her blouse and moved close to the counselor, who having succumbed, began an affair until he finally got Marlene out of the English class with a "withdrawal" instead of an "F" which she should have had. The affair ended at that point.

Marlene had another counselor and another affair next semester.

1. Behavior Is Purposive:

All behavior is produced to achieve an effect. Conversely, all effects produce some behavior.

Effects which control the behavior which produces them are called reinforcers. In the ideal social situations, you and I reciprocally reinforce each other for behavior we desire. Thus, if I help you fix your flat tire, you let me know how grateful you are and that you think I'm "ok" for doing so. In turn, I

62

show you that I am pleased with your appreciation, and on and on it goes.

Looking at it from another point of view, the possibility of punishment also controls my behavior. Walking down the street, I see you struggling with your flat tire problem. I know that if I walk on by, you're going to think badly of me. It's too late to hide, so I take off my coat and lend you a hand. Positive strokes then are applied as before, but my initial reaction was caused by the fear of social punishment.

Situations in which reciprocity is the style are full of mutual positive reinforcement. The subtleness and intricacy of these principles at work make it difficult to analyze them without slicing out and isolating individual events for particular purposes.

The other style of social interaction can be typified by coercion. Coercion describes the condition wherein I must force you to respond to me and you must force me to respond to you.

The mechanism of coercion is not always as subtle as reciprocity, but it can be intricate. The feelings resulting from the coercion model are generally negative, since force and resistance are the two dynamics at play.

Little Michael is trying to show his dad his art work. Dad ignores. Michael then tries to show his mother. Mother is too busy with the evening meal. Michael then tears up his paper. Mom and Dad pay attention, with much consternation. Michael learns that destruction gets attention.

In this example, Michael searches about for the type of behavior that will put him in the limelight. Showing the ark work didn't help. Tearing up the art work did. When saying "please" doesn't get you anywhere, screaming or whining might.

In some living situations, the coercion model becomes predominant. Competing for goodies, both material and non-material, makes people develop strategies which are nonadaptive in dealing with others. Normal social interactions are generally reciprocal. People who develop coercive patterns generally are not comfortable to be with and have difficulty forming long term relationships.

Let's take a look at the two examples we started out with. In Junior's case, he found that talking to adults was a very painful thing. Those to whom he looked for love ignored him until he stuttered. This got some attention for awhile. After adults had taught that stuttering was the right way to talk for attention, they then punished it so extremely that talking to adults at all became non-existent.

Marlene was like many good looking people. She learned to trade upon her charms. To avoid punishment, she could pick up the cues offered by sympathy which gave the green light signal for trading sex for removal of punishment and the provision of protection. While the counselor appeared objective and cool toward her, she was nervous. She saw no way out. When she caught the signal, her only strategy was pulled out of storage and she used it until she got what she wanted.

An additional point to note here is that in each event, a <u>cue</u> was present in addition to payoff. In Junior's case, the presence of an adult cued the promise of pain. In Marlene's case, the vocal and posture changes in the counselor provided the cue for reinforcement (removal of punishment), if she "did her thing." Neither one may have thought it out in so many words. Junior just avoids adults; Marlene thought the counselor was kind of attractive and understanding.

Cues are the traffic lights for behavior. They operate so subtly that we are rarely aware of them.

2. <u>Normal Reactions</u>:

It is a principle of the philosophy of human behavior that all behavior occurs with a certain logic to it. Once you understand it, the behavior makes sense.

The man came to the psychiatrist at the pressure of his friends and relatives. Immediately, the doctor could see the problem: He kept snapping his fingers.

"Why do you snap your fingers?" The doctor inquired.

"It keeps the elephants away!" was the reply.

"There are no elephants around here for miles!" Responded the doctor (who hadn't heard this joke).

"See, Doc, it works!"

Once you understand the behavior, it will make a certain amount of sense.

Your pupils dilate automatically. When there is light, the pupil contracts and when it is darker, the pupil expands to let in more light. It is not thought possible to control this reflex.

64

However, if you ring a bell and simultaneously shine a light on someone's eye, in a short time you will be able to get the pupil to contract by ringing the bell alone.

Were you to exhibit this phenomenon to an uninformed person who knew a little about eye reflexes, it wouldn't seem logical that the eye should respond to an auditory stimulus. But once the full story was known, it would be quite logical.

The behavior we see in children is like the eye reflex to the bell. It is a logical response to an apparently illogical situation. Of course, the behavior patterns of our kids are much more complex, but the principle of logic in behavior still holds true even in the most bizarre of cases.

Actually, the great gurus of psychology and psychiatry are profound because they understand the logic of behavior. They have learned that people behave as they do because it makes sense in some way to behave that way. Believing that the mystifying problem behavior somehow makes sense, they ruminate through a two page list in their heads until they come up with the most probable explanation.

Fight, flight, and grab are three themes in response to stress and frustration. Knowing this may not make you a great psychiatric guru, but it's a beginning.

Fight is a very healthy reaction. It is a stuggle, an "I-won't-be-beaten" attitude that is basically a survival instinct. It is a healthy, normal reaction. But we know it is also unhealthy. If I slug everyone who disagrees with me, I will probably not be too popular.

The first thing we think of in "fight" is usually physical. There are very few kids who are physical to the point where they would kill. They may want to hurt--usually to gain some points in the power game--but it is amazing how often these socio-psychopathic kids back off from seriously injuring anyone.

Verbal aggression is commonly observed in our kids. They have learned to threaten, to call names and to otherwise use verbal means to be aggressive. Sometimes adults are intimidated by this verbal uproar, even the cock-in-the-roost bravado which can be called "posed aggression."

Posed aggression is an artistically orchestrated combination of verbal, postural and gestured threats which can effectively intimidate the average altruistic child care worker. In fact, some kids get the reputation for being really violent without laying a hand on anyone.

Fighting is a normal reaction to aggression and restraint of any kind. It is self defense and a struggle for freedom, and as such, can occur in legitimate and even non-physical ways. We speak of people fighting for their rights, fighting to overcome a handicap, struggling to get ahead, etc. Fighting is a natural and normal reaction.

Whenever an adult got too close to Greg, he doubled up his fists. If they didn't back off, he became very agitated and soon would be in a full-blown rage. This was obviously a response conditioned by past experiences when Greg had to defend himself against aggressive adults. The initial reaction is normal, in view of Greg's past experiences. The fact that it has generalized to all adults is maladaptive, although understandable.

Flight is also a common reaction to stress. Escape is healthy at times, just as fighting is. It is also unhealthy at times when fighting in some form would be more adaptive.

Flight sometimes takes the form of withdrawal. We get the picture of the child curled up in the corner trying to protect himself against all sorts of hostile forces. But there are other forms of flight that are not so obvious. For instance, a person who puts up a protective barrier of words or aloofness to protect against things that he or she can't handle is also engaged—in flight.

Flight may also be from the possibility of failure. In order not to fail, the person will avoid a situation. We sometimes see the child who has been the victim of many placements putting up all kinds of barriers against being close to someone:

"Everyone I ever loved or tried to love has left me or hurt me. I'll never let people hurt me again!" This was said by an angry adult who looked back upon his childhood in which he went through a variety of placements. A lot of our children aren't able to articulate their feelings this well. If they only could, we might learn a lot.

Another phenomenon of children in our care is what I call, "Grab." So many of the children seem to grab attention, food, affection, etc., as if there isn't enough to go around.

The self-centeredness implied in the grab phenomenon makes sense. When you can't count on the people, things and the circumstances of your environment, you have to grab onto things to make them real. All the people, all the food, all the affection you see are yours (and therefore, real) only if you can hold them or control them.

Grab is for the moment, but only the here and now exists for the child. Everything that should remain constant, changes rapidly. Parents are things of the past; brothers and sisters are far away; foster parents and staff have marched by in steady cadence. Only the child him or herself remains constant and thus, self-centeredness makes a lot of sense; it's the only constant in the midst of confusion.

Fight, flight and grab. All three are strategies for self-protection. They protect from the threat of physical assault, psychological pain, and against the chaotic circumstances which occur in the experiences of these children.

3.   Abnormal Situations:

Normal reactions become non-adaptive when they become habitual due to prolonged experience of abnormal situations. We shall consider three main types of abnormal situations: Inconsistency, poor modeling, and deprivations.

Consistency is the basis for a normal development. It means that the child can count on the world because things, people and events are basically dependable. If the environment is dependable, the child can be comfortable with her or himself and can feel free to experiment and explore.

Inconsistency is, of course, the opposite. In the inconsistent world, the child cannot feel at ease to develop and try new things. Acceptance may not be there. The child does not know what will happen if he or she does a certain thing. Some children develop a fight strategy; others develop a flight strategy. Whatever strategy is developed, the child usually has to develop it to an extreme.

In the inconsistent environment, the child finds that parental discipline is not predictable. If it isn't predictable, it can sometimes be manipulated. In fact, it must be manipulated or it becomes more unpredictable and potentially threatening.

Sammy woke up. He had fallen asleep on the couch. The T.V. was still on. Cartoons were flipping over and over on the old set.

After going to the bathroom, Sammy checked the kitchen cabinets. No cereal. He went to the refrigerator. A cold chicken leg made breakfast.

He left the house after finding his tennis shoes.

Shortly after midnight, he returned. Momma was smoking a cigarette in her chair watching through half closed eyes as it displayed a fuzzy old war movie.

"Sammy! You take my ten dollars?"

"No, Momma."

I don't think I spend it. You took it, I think!"

Sammy ignored his mother, went to the refrigerator. Nothing but a quart of beer was in it.

Momma was still yelling as Sammy stomped out the back door. He didn't return until he was sure she was asleep.

Poor modeling is so powerful an influence that it can even overcome the effects of consistency. We learn a great deal from what we observe in people who are powerful, reinforcing, and influential. We pick up attitudes, behavior strategies and idiosyncrasies from observation, mostly without realizing it.

The research in the last few years on the subject of modeling tells us how powerful it is and what a great tool it is for understanding, predicting and changing human behavior.

Professionals in the study of child abuse have long held the axiom that the abusing parent was most likely abused as a child. And, of course, the theme goes on and on and child abuse multiplies at an increasing rate.

Other parental characteristics are also passed on to children. Eating habits are a prime example. Tendencies toward obesity may or may not be genetically inherited, but it is frequently behaviorally inherited through learned eating habits and patterns.

Anger responses are inherited in the same way. Hygiene, grooming, and vocational interests are likewise taught through modeling. It may not always be the parent who is the model, but they were the first models for the child.

People model famous people. If John Wayne walks a certain way, there are sure to be some imitators. Groucho Marx's type of humor caught on and became vogue in living rooms and parties, as well as night clubs all over.

More concrete evidence is being accumulated that television and movies influence and exert control over the behavior of viewers, young and old alike. The effects of observing the violent heroes and anti-heroes is reflected in the newspapers with alarming predictability. The old belief that such things are "cathartic" has not only been proven wrong, but dangerous.

The influence of the criminal, whether pimp or whore, is prevalent in the "street culture." These roles can be presented as successful to the youngster growing up in the "street culture."

Another abnormal situation is deprivation. Some very interesting studies done with maternal deprivation in animals at an early age show a great many interesting things. These studies, so far as we can relate them to the human animal, help us understand the influence of early development. Lack of maternal contact as babies leads to inability of deprived monkeys to relate when they are adults.

Thus far, there is sufficient reason to believe early environmental influences are extremely powerful and may not be totally correctable.

Ask the generation that was young during the depression. They'll tell you that you don't throw things away, you clean your plate, etc. Financial deprivation leaves its marks just as emotional deprivation does.

(One fallacy in this concept is that deprivation of food at an early age produces adult overeating. People who were so deprived may overeat, undereat, or have weird eating habits, but so do people who have not been deprived. Whatever causes a problem initially does not maintain the problem today. The reason it is a problem today far outweighs the significance of whatever started the mess in the first place.)

Nutritional and health anomalies are, of course, a serious concern. Sometimes they can be corrected or ameliorated; often they can't be. The effects of such problems in the critical growth years can have monumental repercussions throughout life.

No matter what the abnormal situation, it is the task of child care to restore (often really create) normalcy. A normal person can adjust to most situations which life presents, despite handicaps. This ability seems to arise from a central core of security.

4. Abnormal Reactions:

Kids are referred to us because they behave abnormally. Some people who were too long in school give us labels to help us set these kids apart from ourselves and the people we love. We are normal, they are abnormal. They are insane, we are sane. We are adjusted, they are maladjusted. They are disturbed, we are only turbed. Mainly, they are labelled, and we are not.

The intent of this chapter has been to show that these kids respond in understandable ways to abnormal situations. As a result of this habitual pattern of responses, the child transfers to what then become abnormal reactions to normal situations. Then the kid gets the label.

The transition from the abnormal situation to the normal is known technically as "generalization." This is the behavioral term which describes the phenomenon in which the same behavior occurs in responses to a variety of cues ("discriminative stimuli," if you want to impress someone).

The way it works is simply like this: Uncle Marty has a big nose. Little Suanne is the apple of his eye. When she hugs him, Uncle Marty gives her a nickel. In the future, Suanne may _generalize_ to all men with big noses and she will probably feel affection toward them.

The same holds true for painful experiences. If authority people have been inconsistent and mean, the child is likely to mistrust and fear authority people in the future.

As the child is pinballed through placements, a large number of subtle cues are being formed to which the child develops particular responses. These responses may have initially been adaptive, but in new situations, they become maladaptive.

If we could put these cues and their responses into sentences, we might better grasp and deal with them. For example:

"Criticism is a personal attack, I'd better attack back to defend myself."

"Affection is a prelude to pain, avoid it."

"Physicians hurt me, kick them in the groin."

"If a girl is friendly, she wants sex."

70

"Social workers make child care workers leave you alone, so be nice to the social worker."

"Avoid new experiences because they make you look dumb and people laugh at you."

"If I give you sex, you'll like me."

One of the qualities that can break down the connection between some of these cues and their consequent responses is the building of trust. In addition, there should be a multitude of experiences which disconfirm the generalizations.

Trust is especially indicated because it is the breakdown of the cue-response connection regarding frustrating experiences with adults. The trust breakthrough comes only through consistency in both objective events and general behavior of the adults in the environment. All authority is not pernicious, but this must be repeatedly demonstrated.

The other generalizations can be broken after the trust is built. Having built the trust, the child is ready to hear you explain that some of the maladaptions are what they are and the child can break even more connections.

5. Resolution:

It is repeated throughout this book that consistency is a solution to many of the problems our children have. It is not, of course, the only answer, but it provides a solid ground upon which to build normalization.

It comes down to this: The child can only form a clear idea of who he is, who others are and the relationship between them if the environment is stable and energy need not be expended upon attempts to protect and control, to fight, take flight, and grab.

Modeling is another powerful tool for changing children's behavior. But to be a model, you must be responded to by the child as a model. No matter how much you say you are a model, you aren't unless the child is imitating you.

To be a model, you must not have too great a distance between you and the child. A black girl from the slums is not likely to find a rich lady from Bolivia as her model. That's extreme, but true. There must not be too great a difference. They have to see that they could be like you someday.

You also have to be powerful or highly respected by people the child sees as significant. Just because you are from the same neighborhood doesn't mean that you are a model. The pimp is a prime example of a model. (He's cool!)

Modeling plus instruction is a double barrelled approach. Once the consistency is established and the trust is built and modeling is evident (Does the kid scratch his head like you do? That's a sure sign!), instructing the kid in appropriate behavior can be effective. (A little instruction, falling like the dew from heaven, not like a flood from a backed-up toilet.)

The model is the best instructor, but instructing needs to be done carefully so as not to lecture, and should start where the kids is.

Practice makes perfect. You can't learn a practical art by talking or reading. Eventually, you have to try it, fail and try it again. Once the conceptual framework is laid down with the kid in his or her own language, the next step is to try it out. Get them to practice, to try to break the cue connections that limit their possibilities in life. Talk it out, act it out, and act it out again.

The above may sound a lot like "therapy." Child care workers who make it as models can make it as informal counselors if they don't try to bend the relationship too much.

CHAPTER 8

EXPLOSIVE SITUATIONS

Violence is attractive. It draws spectators, sells soap and padded bras; it finances multi-million dollar movie studios. It also scares people and revolts them—but they still watch it.

Plato noted this strange phenomenon in The Republic. Torn between revulsion and attraction, we find attraction winning, and most of us gravitate toward it, and it is twice as attractive because it is forbidden.

At the time of this writing, the psychological and sociological studies on violence are just beginning to be taken seriously by politicians and educators. The studies on violence show that observing violence produces violence. Television and movies were at first believed to be "cathartic" in that violent "id impulses" could be vicariously drained off by observing violence. Research, however, has not supported that thesis. On the contrary, modeling tends to produce imitation of what is observed rather than to defuse inner explosive tendencies.

Some recent sociological studies show that to an alarming degree, children are learning violence at home. They see it used by their parents as a means of responding to problems and frustrations. These children are doubly victimized because they are both abused and subjected to exceedingly powerful learning experiences which they will tend to use in the future when they encounter frustration or situations wherein they will have to deal with their own anger.

The picture emerging is not an optimistic one. The mass media, entertainment, as well as parents and the community are all in synergistic concert creating a society that is breeding violence at an epidemic rate.

The remedies for this are not foreseen. The news media feels it is their obligation to give us detailed news on hijacking, mass murders, and war. Entertainment media find it lucrative to produce violence and often try to justify it by saying that the good guy wins in the end. (Studies show this probably has little effect on the learning process.) Unless something is done on a large scale to change things, and done very soon, we will find that violence is actually going to become "as American as apple pie."

With this depressing scenario in mind, let us look at what that means in child care. Child care, as such, is not in the business of changing the whole of society in any large sense. Hopefully, we are all willing to do what we can to see that society becomes a better place in which to live, but we have the obligation to deal with society's ill effects on a case by case basis.

The first case we have to deal with is us. Violence is like sex. It is so much a part of our culture that we cannot deny it to make it go away. It has to be faced squarely.

It was hard not to tell John, "I told you so!" He came to child care loudly proclaiming that he was peaceful, that he believed in Gandhi and non-violence. In three weeks, he had slugged a kid.

Consider also the case of Ben, a very religious administrator and gentle giant of a man who rarely came into contact with the children. One day something of a riot occurred and Ben happened to be on the scene. He explained what happened in his deep, but gentle voice: "Joe seemed to be the leader and he came at me with a bat in his hand. I said a prayer to the Lord for guidance and picked him up and slammed him against the wall. I didn't let him go until he promised to settle down, about five seconds." I could imagine Ben doing all of this very calmly and actually without losing control. John, however, really lost control. Neither of them ever intended to use violence to solve problems. But violence is learned regardless of its intentions.

There is a myth we must learn to dispell from our heads: Intellectual learning is a very weak way to learn skills. Intent is also weak. Thus, John's avowed pacifism is a weak deterent to acting violently. He espoused non-violence intellectually and, if it had never been tested as kids can test it, he would have never learned a valuable lesson about himself.

A great many behaviors are learned without intending to learn them. The speed at which we eat, for example, is learned without much thought. Our general outlooks on life are also conditioned over years in very subtle ways.

Violence is learned that way. We see it used for solving problems by parents, older siblings, the police and TV heroes and

74

villains. Without realizing what is happening, we learn our lessons well and we will tend to use our lessons unless we succeed in counteracting them through purposive, controlled practice.

That is the remedy. Some psychotherapists have demonstrated, through programmed role playing, that violent tendencies can be weakened. People can also program themselves to handle violence by imagining the possible explosive situations and themselves handling it calmly. It is more effective to do it with other people and act it out realistically.

Cues are another important aspect in understanding violence. Again, without realizing it, we associate certain aspects of the environment with certain moods, feelings and behavior. The cue can be virtually anything that can be sensed. It need not be consciously noticed to be a cue, nor is it necessary that an apparent connection be seen between the cue and the behavior.

A cue signals a behavior. It says "go ahead," and "time to act." Saying "no" to someone may trigger a tantrum, or a whine or a cooing sound: "Ah, please, Jerry, just this once."

A cue may be a very subtle thing. It can signal "no" as well as "yes." An employee wants a raise. He gains an interview with his boss. "Before we settle down to talk about your business, I want to call your attention to the monthly reports. They are a bit shoddy lately." That changes the employee's topic.

More subtly, you walk in to see about a raise. You walk out without asking for it. You aren't sure why you didn't ask. Something just told you not to do so. Somewhere in that interview you realized it was no good to ask. It could be a furrowed brow, a bit of posture or something else that signalled to you that it was the wrong time.

Violence is often cued by previous experiences the person has had that mean one of two things: Violence will pay off; or I am cornered and have to fight my way out. The cue might be confrontation or it might be catching someone in the act of doing something wrong. It could be the presence of peers when "face" must be saved or "macho" must be established.

In any event, psychology tells us that there is a reason for the behavior. Past experience, modeling and cues are to be taken into account in understanding violence. In child care, we need to deal with this problem. Some agencies will not tolerate the violent child; but this child needs to be helped. His or her violent behavior finds the child as the greatest victim.

1. Examples:

Bruce was fourteen when I met him. He was 5'10" and very strong for his age. He had been through many male staff. Several of whom he had personally sent on to other careers, licking their wounds.

His pattern was as follows: He would set up or find himself in a situation where a male staff had to confront him. Then he would explode and attack the staff. His reputation depended upon his driving the staff off.

The end of Bruce's reign of terror came when a new program was established. Twice he attacked the newest male staff person and twice this staff person came back and said: "Bruce, it won't work. You can't drive me off!" Bruce gave up on this project, tried the next new staff male and finally gave up. Bruce finally got his own head together and was successfully returned to his mother.

Chuck was only thirteen, but he was a terror. He wasn't big enough to successfully attack staff, but he was violent. He liked to use weapons to even up the chances.

One day Chuck was on the roof of a building. Several staff and kids watched as George climbed up to get him safely down. Chuck was armed with two knife shaped pieces of broken glass. Down on the ground the staff herded the kids away.

No audience. Chuck threatened with his weapons. George said, "Nice day, isn't it? I think I'll enjoy the sun up here with you for awhile." Chuck was silent.

Soon Chuck dropped the glass in the right hand. "Well, I guess it's time to go down and go to work. I'll see you later," George said.

Chuck said, "Wait!" (Dropping the other piece of glass.) "I'm scared up here. Help me down."

Chuck would have been forced to be violent and someone would have gotten hurt if the audience had remained. Alone, he could admit he was scared of heights and there was no disgrace in letting his hostile front drop. George was careful not to force Chuck into a position where he had to "save face" and go down fighting.

John was a bluffer. It is interesting that he had the reputation for being violent but never had been know to be violent.

He was a very successful bluffer. He was an expert at never challenging when he would have to follow through.

Staff learned his game and, for better or worse, decided to play along. It was John's style to never challenge a staff person when he would be confronted and staff would always let him play "tough guy" as long as it didn't interfere with the routines or the interests of the other kids.

John was seventeen, and staff decided that the "tough guy" act could be tolerated until he was eighteen and out on his own. This was probably a mistake. Behind the "tough guy" mask was a frightened kid who couldn't cope with a lot of the problems of growing up. He needed a chance to learn to make and be a friend. The "tough guy" only had intimidated followers.

2. Analysis of Violent Kid/Situations:

The violent child will always be with us. More and more, child care agencies will have to be prepared to treat such children because violence is becoming an increasing problem in our society.

The first step in treating any problem is to analyze it. It follows the scientific method in gathering data, stating the hypothesis and evaluating the results.

When we deal with kids, the best source of data is the child. What does he or she say in his or her pattern of behavior:

Staff: "You ever blow your cool, Sandy?"

Sandy: "Once in a while I had to let my Old Lady know she wasn't boss over me."

Staff: "She really pushed you around, eh?"

Sandy: "One time she told me my friend couldn't stay over at our house. Ma had her friends over and I couldn't. So we fought."

Staff: "How did you fight?"

Sandy: "She yelled, I yelled. Then we started pushing and then hitting. The neighbors finally called the cops."

Staff: "Then what happened?"

Sandy: "The cops came and separated us. We cooled down later and they left."

Staff: "What about your friend?"

Sandy: "I told her to go home. I guess I didn't want her to stay after all."

What do we learn from this conversation? Sandy's pattern in this instance is: Set up conflict, fight, then give in. What did she gain from it? Possibly she just wanted to get her mother's attention or to embarrass her in front of others (neighbors, police).

Another source of data from the child is what we and others have observed. We need to analyze these observations in terms of cue, behavior and consequences.

Cue. What was done or said before the explosion? Who was present? What issues were brought up before the situation erupted?

Behavior. Explosive situations are like roller coaster rides. They start out at the normal level, accelerate to a peak and then drop back to the normal level again. Describe this acceleration. What happened as the child left the level of normalcy and reached the peak? How rapid is the ascent? How broad is the peak; i.e., how long does the child stay at the peak? How rapidly did the child descend to the normal level? Is there more than one peak at the top? What happens to signal the descent?

Derrick refused to pick up the dinner dishes. He was told he couldn't leave the dining room until he did so. Staff stood at each doorway. He swore, pushed, grabbed a chair and threw it against a wall. Next he turned over a table. Finally, he took a swing at a staff person. By this time, he was breathing in short shallow breaths and was in a rage.

When he took the swing, staff had to restrain him. He fought for awhile and then calmed down, did his chore and voluntarily went to his room.

You can see the pattern in Derrick's behavior. The physical aggression against staff was his peak. From this example, it looks like he depended upon this act to get someone to control him. Whatever was the dynamic, we see the acceleration process quite clearly. The climb was slow in the beginning, then rapid, with a sharp peak and rapid descent to normalcy.

With some kids, the peak can continue for days. With most, it will be over quickly, but it may reach the normal level only after several days of upset and minor flare-ups.

78

Consequence. Did the behavior occur for some outcome? What pay off did the child expect or get for the violence? In the past, was there an inconsistent consequence for the violent behavior that would not always occur, but lock the child into a strong habit through intermittent reinforcement?

Hold on, let me explain. Behaviors become strong habits when they get their pay offs inconsistently. It is like the gambler who wins enough to keep him playing, although he loses more often. It is the winning every now and then that keeps him going. Experiments in this type of pay off system prove that you can make an occasional behavior habitual the less often it is reinforced. I mentioned this because it contradicts "common sense" which views the compulsive gambler as desiring to lose and the violent person as wanting to be controlled. Intermittent reinforcement makes a better hypothesis in most cases and should be ruled out before proceeding to another explanation.

What are some pay offs? Violence may be used to get: Attention, physical contact, revenge, material possessions, privileges, or prestige. It can be used to avoid: Losing face, being accused, losing friends, losing material possessions and to avoid physical and psychological threat.

It is sometimes very difficult to decide what pay off is sought through violence. This is because it can occur for multiple reasons and because of the nature of intermittent reinforcement.

Rage. Sometimes a child will become so violent that control is totally gone. Usually this comes from panic reaction on the part of the child. Like a cornered animal, the child is lashing out in fear for his or her life. Sometimes the rage starts out as aggression, but fear of reprisal, based on past experience, sets in and what was an attack becomes a defense although the difference may not be readily apparent at the time.

Premeditated violence. The same motivations exist but the child never loses control. He or she thinks out the plan, usually to get even for something or to drive away staff.

Once you have analyzed the violence, you can set out some hypotheses about what provokes it and about how to bring it under control. We can approach violence control in two ways. The first way is to control whether or not it happens.

James had been in a mental hospital and was diagnosed as psychotic. He was extremely sensitive about that and you could expect an explosion if anyone called or implied he was "crazy."

You could control his outbursts by avoiding that word or implication.

The other kind of control is self control. People will never learn to control themselves if they are sheltered from stress. Thus, in treatment planning, it is logical to have violent people exposed to explosive stimuli in order for them to learn control.

If at first your hypothesis about what will work fails, don't be too proud to look at it a second time and try something different. Something will work. You only have to find the correct technique.

3. How To Prevent Violence:

While we have to face violence to treat it, we need not create it as a standard bill of fair. No kid, no matter how violent, wants to be involved in turmoil at all times. Our best tool is, again, structure and consistency.

It occurs with amazing frequency that real hell raising brats come into a consistent environment and turn in their horns for halos. (Well, almost.) Violence may have been the child's way for getting attention or other goodies. In a therapeutic atmosphere, the old weapons can be laid aside because they serve no purpose.

Structure and consistency are our best tools and they are absolutely essential prerequisites for any kind of treatment.

Beyond the basics you can let the child know from day one that there is no place for violence in this program. Explain that it isn't worth it; it doesn't pay. Explain the consequences of violence if it should occur and explain that you won't give up because of violence.

The factors involved in relationship are also preventative. If staff establish a relationship with a kid and both have an investment, the likelihood that violence will occur is diminished.

The factors in the relationship include trust, caring, and reciprocity. Trust means that the child feels that the staff will not hurt him or her. It also means that the staff will not allow the child to be hurt. Reciprocally, the child is trusted by the staff person, and the child does not want to break that trust once it develops.

Caring means that the child feels that the staff is concerned about him or her personally. This caring is also something the child does not want to violate, and the child knows that violence may violate the caring and eventually it may be withdrawn. Staff must try to communicate that no matter what, they will still care for the child and it is a really personal thing.

Until the caring is actually grasped by the child, staff will appear to be just staff and the caring will be seen as the staff's job, and that feeling maximizes violence instead of diminishing it.

Reciprocity cuts across both dimensions. It means the staff and the child are giving and taking in care, trust, play, work, etc. When a child comes this far, other treatment is relatively easy.

4. How To Defuse Violence:

Jan was "off the wall." She had broken a window, torn down the drapes, busted a chair and was standing against the wall with a butter knife and a spoon threatening to kill everyone in the house.

A male and female staff stood in front of her, and the other kids were peering out from the dining room to see what was going to happen.

"You can't kill anyone with a butter knife," Greg said.

"You don't know, you dumb hick!"

"The knife isn't sharp. Are you going to butter one of us? And what do you think you can do with that spoon?" Joyce replied.

"Shut up, bitch! I'll kill you first!"

"Don't call Joyce a bitch!" Greg shouted. He was losing his patience.

This went on for about an hour. Jan hurled a threat, Joyce or Greg reasoned or ridiculed. Finally, Jan lunged at them flailing arms and weapons. No one was hurt, and Jan was physically restrained for about thirty minutes and went sullenly to her room.

The first rule of dealing with violence is don't reason, don't argue. The second one is don't ridicule.

The most important thing is to avoid irritating the situation. When you are irrational, you hate to have someone hit you

81

with rationality. The kid isn't thinking or he wouldn't get into that situation.

Be sure you gain control of the situation. Someone has to get control. In most cases, the kid seems to have it. In the case above, Jan had control, but she didn't know what to do with it. Staff found themselves at a loss and waited for her move. Finally, Jan had to make them take control by lunging at them.

You can take control by making the environment safe. Remove all objects that can hurt anyone. Get the other kids engaged in something else so they won't join in, be hurt, or form an audience pro or con.

"Never close a door without opening a window." This old saying means that you don't leave the child without a way out, preferably, with some dignity.

Try to remain calm at all times. No matter what the child does or says, you maintain control by showing the child that you aren't upset and you can deal with whatever happens.

In some cases, you keep talking. This is done to show the child how calm you are. When you are silent, the child may feel more threatened than when you talk. Talk calmly in a quiet tone that stirs little excitement.

While you are talking, don't threaten. Don't make an issue of the consequences or the damage done. If the child mentions them: "You'll make me stay in my room!" say, "Everyone has to abide by the rules," and go on talking in a soothing manner.

When you see the child is regaining composure, suggest some change. "We could go outside for awhile, and if you want to bring your weapons, that's ok." Or you could sit down and show the child you are relaxed in some way. Above all, communicate calmness while never ceasing to be alert.

At times, you may be able to leave the situation. If the child is threatening you, you may find that the issue is not that you confront back, but that you show that you consider the physical confrontation to be a game you don't care to play. So you get busy with something else.

The shock value in this technique is very disarming at times. "Oh, Doug, I have to make out the shopping list, then we'll talk about your problem!" Doug was getting all hot and agitated for a fight and you postponed it to deal with a business issue. It works, sometimes.

82

Remember, part of the violent act involves hooking you into it. Sometimes you can't avoid it. You have to protect people and property, so you must step in when they are in danger. But just because a kid starts to agitate against you doesn't mean you have to play his game.

There may be times when you find that you need help. A self defense course should be provided staff so that you can be fairly self sufficient without calling in outside help.

Outside help irritates the explosive situation. But if it is beyond control, you may have no other choice. It is best that we avoid calling the police, but in some cases, they are the only ones who can do the job. Agency policies should provide guidelines in such cases.

Many explosive situations can be prevented by admitting that we can be wrong. Child care workers, like children, are not perfect. There are many times when we take a negotiable issue and make it the battleground for a power struggle.

Don't excuse yourself too quickly from this common failure. It happens in every kind of human endeavor. When you have authority you feel you must use it and you tend to view any questioning of your power as a personal attack and threat to your control.

Staff decided that Bonnie (age 16), should exercise daily to help her lose weight. At first, Bonnie agreed. After a week of jogging in place for fifteen minutes per day, she got bored and refused to do it. The resulting confrontation turned into a full blown explosion which, in turn, raised issues which extended for weeks.

Was this a negotiable issue? At Bonnie's age, it certainly was. Anyone sixteen years old has more negotiable issues than they did when they were ten. The dimensions of power must change to recognize this.

5. **After the Storm:**

After the battle is over, much work needs to be done. You need to immediately renew your commitment to the kid, you may need to deal with the child's guilt or shame, and you need to start over.

Put yourself in the child's place. The fight is over. He or she (hopefully) didn't win. Has he lost your concern and trust? Is he going to be pinballed out of this agency? Will his parents find out? Will you talk about him?

83

A violent episode should be considered a matter of the highest confidentiality. Except for the necessary reports, it should be kept between you and the child. Assure him or her of that.

It is time for a lot of assurance now. Don't sound apologetic and don't say, "Oh, that's all right, Roberta!" It isn't all right. It was wrong for everyone and especially for Roberta because it is another failure. But it is over. Let's pay the consequences, clean up the mess and begin life again.

You should think in this pattern: Explosion, control, consequences and back to normal. By the time you get the situation back to normal, the issue is closed. Don't drag it out needlessly to put the kid down.

Finally, a word about therapy. Very little has been accomplished in traditional therapy regarding the resolution of violence. More promise lies in role playing techniques which follow the model proposed by Albert Bandura in his book, **Aggression**.

There are no deep secrets about the use of such techniques. You can use them if you have gained the confidence of the child, and if you can get some commitment to change from him or her. That isn't easy.

The following is a suggested model for gaining the commitment:

1. Help the person realize that violence isn't productive and stands in the way of being a normal person.

2. Suggest that he or she can learn to use self control.

3. Start now.

Start what? There are three techniques that can be used separately or in combination:

First technique:

1. Review a typical recent incident step by step.

2. Have the child go through the scenario verbally and tell what he or she could have done to prevent it.

Second technique:

1. As number 1 above.

2. Discuss better ways to handle such situations.

3.   Role play the better ways with:

    a.   first you play the kid's part

    b.   then the kid plays him or herself

4.   Role play a variety of similar situations.

Third technique:

1.   As numbers 1 and 2 above.

3.   Assign the kid to purposefully get into similar real situations with the intent of actually controlling self.

4.   Have the child report back to you on progress daily.

It is not the staff's job to be therapists, but they are often the best people to do the job. In fact, when you think about it, you really are the therapists, and you must be prepared to deal with a variety of problems in a variety of ways. That is not just an aphorism, it is a future trend.

CHAPTER 9

GOALS, OBJECTIVES, MEANS, PLANS AND DUMB LUCK

When Uncle Rod's wheat farm was eaten by sheep, he started a sheep farm.

When the sheep were eaten by wolves, he started a wolf farm.

When the wolves were stunk out by skunks, he started a skunk farm.

Finally, the skunks ran off and Uncle Rod died—and started a worm farm.*

Uncle Rod was a planner, but he was also an opportunist. When things did not go his way, he went the way things went. Treatment planning is like that. You plan with what you have available and have to be flexible enough to take advantage of any turn of events.

1. What Is a Treatment Plan?

A treatment plan is a purposive statement in response to a need which establishes goals, the means to be used and a technique to evaluate the plan.

Now, that sounds really stale and formal doesn't it? Well, let me put some sugar on this medicine and see if it goes down a little easier.

If you tell me you are going to get rich someday, I may believe you, but I really won't take you seriously. I may believe you are tired of beans and beer and would like steak and

---

*For a better version of a similar story, see e. e. cummings: "Nobody loses all the time." The Complete Poems of e. e. cummings, 1913-1962. Harcourt, Brace, Jovanovich, Inc., New York, 1972.

champagne, but I don't seriously see you getting anywhere with your wishes. You're dreaming.

Now, if you tell me you are going to save half your salary, invest it in a year along with the proceeds from the sale of the small farm you own and so forth, I am inclined to take you more seriously. Why?

First of all, you got more specific. You started talking about how you were going to get rich.

Suppose you say to me, "I want to live in a house in Buck-flash Acres. Insurance executives live there, so I'm going to join Dad's firm as a vice-president and in two years, I'll be there." Now, I think that's a believable plan. Instead of "get rich" as your goal, you have become even more specific about what you mean by that. If I ask you, you will add that you want that new $25,000 Drinque Gasse sports car to park in the driveway. And where will you buy your shoes? Your clothes? Etc?

A purposive plan is specific. We don't take your plan to get rich seriously if you just dream. We aren't going to think much of your treatment plan if it is just a dream. And a treatment plan is for people--"rich" is only money.

A treatment plan sets out what we propose to accomplish. We have to get that firmly in mind. The purpose, the goal--these things set the whole direction for what we are going to do. Does the end justify the means? If it doesn't, nothing else will!

Your purpose will justify what you do. The purpose specifies the goal, from the goal come your objectives and from your objectives come the things you do to reach them.

Be careful not to lose sight of your goals and objectives when you decide on the means. You do not propose to use "therapy" to help a child unless you have firmly established the goals and objectives first and no other means seems feasible.

The means you use are further prescribed by three considerations which are time, resources, and ethics.

Time works against us in many cases. How much time do we have to work with a child--a year, six months, three weeks? Time will limit how much we can do and help us set priorities based upon the tension between what needs to be done and what we have time to accomplish. Sometimes the "big" problems must be left unresolved due to the amount of time available.

Resources also play a vital part in setting objectives. Vocational, educational and other resources of the community impose a limit on what can be done. If a child needs a special training program and it doesn't exist, and we can't construct one, we are stuck. Thus, while we should think of the ideal, we must, at last, come down to the real when we make a treatment plan.

Ethics, of course, dictate that we cannot violate rights as we treat. We cannot torture or use any cruel or unusual means to achieve a desirable goal.

Evaluation is the most important aspect of treatment planning. If we are producing change, we must be prepared to measure it. We must be accountable.

Some people say that what we do can't be measured. This was a common statement in social services until recently. Even now, there are many "professionals" who staunchly assert that what they do can't be measured. They and they alone will determine whether their therapy is successful or not.

Such stone age thinking ignores the fact that the public pays for change and if they pay for it, they want to know it has happened and the change they are concerned about had better be noticeable to others.

When children are referred to us, we have a serious obligation to account for what we do and the results. Children come with problems a, b, and c. When they leave, they should leave without them or with a measurable decrease in them which will assure us of optimum adjustment to society.

We come down to this: A treatment plan is essential; it specifies goals, objectives, means and evaluation. An example can be stated thus:

Goal: Return John (age 12) to this family in one year.

Objectives:

1.   John will control his temper; i.e., in situations in which he does not get his way—is told no—or otherwise frustrated, he will accept it without visible evidence of anger for a period of one month.

2.   Etc.

3.   Etc.

Evaluation: As measured by criteria stated above, as recorded in log.

2. Problems:

Before we set goals, we have to identify some problems. A problem is some behavior we want to increase, decrease, or maintain. That may sound simple. (It is, at least conceptually.)

We want to increase things like politeness, personal hygiene, school attendance, etc. If we apply a graph to these things, we want to see an increase in frequency during some sort of observation.

Some things we will define as needing to be decelerated. Examples of such things include fighting, runaways, stealing, manipulation, lying, and a host of other maladaptive behaviors which stand in the way of moving toward independence.

Maintenance is seen as a problem when a new improvement has not had time to solidify. Attaining a goal is not as important as solidifying it. Right? And it takes time to make sure the temporary gain doesn't become just a flash in the pan which is quickly lost. It took a long time to develop and maintain the problem, so let's make sure that we maintain the progress a sufficient amount of time before we start cheering.

An important aspect of understanding problems is the ownership question. Who owns the problem? Is it the child's problem? Who labelled it as his or her problem? Is it the family's problem? Is it the system that created and maintained the problem?

It is rare for the problem to originate with the child, but origin and ownership are two different things. By the time the child has developed habits of maladaption, the problems are hers or his and origin becomes irrelevant.

Ownership implies responsibility. If I have a problem, no matter where I got it, I can't blame anyone for it because I, and I alone, must solve it and if I don't, and don't seek help, I accept the problem.

This line of thinking doesn't occur to most children, of course, and the children are placed because we are accustomed to making such decisions for them and even they expect we will take responsibility from them.

The child's family may have the problem. We sometimes find that the child has no problems when he or she is placed away from the family. Conclusion: the family maintained the problems.

How does this happen? A lot of psychologists can tell you, but basically, we observe that when the social-family constellation is altered, the behavior is changed. The situation needed treatment.

The converse is also true: When the child is removed, sometimes the family functions better. This may not mean that the child was the main problem. Again, when you remove the child, the constellation of roles, expectations and contingencies changes.

To those of you who are anti-establishment weirdos, blaming "the system" is not new. You can't blame "them" or "it" all of the time. The system may be messed up, but alternatives are not better. Anyhow, let's give the system some credit as well as the blame. It so richly deserves both.

Probably the first thing wrong with the system (of which we are a part) is that it thrives on the problem and in no way can "solve" it. There is not hope that at some magic day down the road the last child will be placed and the last screwed up family will be unscrewed and we will all go retire to Burn Out Villa in Fort Mosquito, Florida, to live out our waning years reminiscing like the old soldiers do.

Child care, public and private, will not solve the problem by the case by case method. Something larger is needed, and needed badly, because the problem is growing not diminishing.

There are system characteristics of the problems with which we deal. The first one of note is labelling. In order to convince those who hold the purse strings that a child should be placed, a case must be made for the placement. If not a psychiatric label, at least a description of incorrigible behavior which the kid owns and must be treated.

Socially, the child brokerage system deals in children from the lower socio-economic status. It is rare (unheard of) that they take guardianship from middle or upperclass parents. Minority groups are overrepresented among the placement kids.

Multiple placements create further problems. Children who are pinballed through the public and private system learn to work out a kind of adjustment to that crazy state of affairs. But the strategies you develop to adjust to craziness do not help you adjust to the normal state of affairs.

Treatment plans designed to combat the system problems involve stability (you don't let the kid crazy her or himself out of the program), consistency (you create a dependable environment) and caring (you don't reject the kid for messing up).

3. Goals:

There is a poster that says, "If you don't know where you're going, you'll probably end up somewhere else." We are so used to floating along through the drain pipe of life that we forget that we could make some goals and actually alter some courses. We won't alter our course or anyone else's without taking the time to define the goals.

In treatment planning, we need to consider three kinds of goals. They are long term, short term, and tentative.

The long term or long range goal is the most important goal because it gives direction to the others. A long term goal is a goal that we will expect to accomplish in a period of time which may be up to several years away.

Long term goals are tied to logical time periods. A long term goal may be tied to graduation, completing a course of training, a birthdate in the future or some other event. In child care, we usually pin the long term goal onto the date of planned discharge from the program.

Long range goals are achievable wishes which are governed by the real on one hand and the possible on the other. They set out a future desirable situation, with a date attached, in specific enough description that its accomplishment is unquestionable when it is accomplished.

In treatment planning, the long term goal will describe that state of relevant events which will characterize the individual when she or he has reached the planned discharge date.

Which of the following is a good goal statement?

1. When John leaves the program, he will be good.

2. When John leaves the program, he will have a good self image.

3. When John leaves the program, he will have gained control of his temper, have learned a skill and will be able to hold a job.

4. John won't leave the program.

5. Who is John?

I would guess that #3 is the best goal statement. (I do think the idiot who wrote it should have given a date for when John will leave the program.)

Goal statements can be general, but should not be vague. John being good is vague. Good to eat? Good to look at? Good for nothing? What does it mean? Good, bad, nice, pretty, sucessful, etc. are vague terms and are all bad.

General terminology gives us a class of events. To "learn a skill" is a class statement. "To learn to do auto body work" is more specific and better. Depending upon the circumstances, the more specific the statement, the better when setting up the long term goals.

Short term goals are generally set for periods within the limits of the long term goals. If you establish a one year goal, you may set up a short term goal for one month or two or six or eight months. Example:

Long Term Goal--At completion of the program, Georgia will have mastered sufficient clerical skills to get a job in an office (two years).

Short Term Goal--In the next six months, Georgie will improve her typing from 42 correct words per minute to 50.

Short term goals are related to the accomplishment of the long term goal as subgoals. Short term goals can also be unrelated. Georgia may decide to clear up her acne in a month, which has nothing to do with clerical skills, but is important for other reasons.

Tentative goals are generally established to provide some directed thinking before the plan can be consolidated. These are set before the child is placed or (take note) at a time when the child is not available for co-planning. Later, they are refined.

(That is an important point to bear in mind. We can sit in offices or anywhere and make all kinds of plans for kids, but they won't work without the co-planning by the kid. After all, it's the kid's life.)

Goal setting is an exercise in deductive logic. We go from the general to the particular in the goal setting process so that we don't become like the guy in the saying: "After losing sight of his goals, he redoubled his efforts." Without the goals, we can flounder about, playing mind games on ourselves and on the kids; and that isn't ethical!

4. Objectives:

After we have gone through the strain of establishing the goals, we get down to the business of setting objectives. This is where we really get measurable.

An objective is a goal in particular. It sets out the measurable, time defined subgoal in terms that make it unquestionable as to whether it is accomplished or not.

The objective has four characteristics: It describes the behavior (or result of the behavior) specifically; it labels the conditions under which the behavior is to be observed; it sets out the criteria for the achievement of the objective; and it states the time for its completion.

While eating, Philomena will not stuff her mouth to the point at which she cannot talk. After 100% of this behavior has been observed at each meal over a period of two months, this objective will be deemed a success.

Another statement could be: Marcella will not wet her bed for three months.

I will quit smoking. After six months, I'll consider it a success and set another objective.

Every Sunday evening, I will write my mother a letter. I'll keep this up for four months to establish the habit.

I will respond to 80% of the directives given me by the boss within two days. (I threw a curve this time. Criteria are not over time, but in percentage.)

5. Means:

When we don't have the ends in mind, we see people ardently playing with things which are means. When the long term goal is absent, all sorts of irrelevant things happen. Kids get therapied, they get programmed, they fall victim to every imaginable form of brain tinkering.

But with the goal in mind, tinkering becomes therapy because it makes sense as a means toward that terminal goal. Also, certain means will become blatantly irrelevant if they don't relate to a goal or objective.

Motivation is a many faceted concept and phenomenon. Motivation is what we see when we observe someone who wants something.

People who are described as "motivated" are obvious in the purposiveness of their behavior. Others may be motivated, but their motivation is not so obvious.

Another way to look at motivation is in terms of reinforcement or payoff. People will do certain things to obtain certain reinforcers. A hungry person will do almost anything for food, an alcoholic will do almost anything for a drink, and a new social worker will do almost anything to make a client grateful.

Sometimes the reinforcement is not so simple and direct. Thus, a young lady may want to get married. She'll do anything, including love some man to get that status.

People are also motivated by fear, to avoid punishment or pain. The student may work hard, not so much to get good grades as to avoid all of the social stigma and other consequences attached to not getting good grades.

In treatment planning, it is seldom that the long term goal is so compelling as to motivate a lot of consistent performance. Objectives may be motivating, but sometimes that is not enough either. In the event that accomplishment isn't sufficient motivation, extraneous contingencies must be applied.

The objective states that, "Eric will do his homework every evening on which it is assigned for a minimum of one hour." Eric may have no motivation to do so. Staff must step in and make a set of contengencies which may include: No T.V., praise, snacks, attention, and on and on.

Resources involved in the means include people and material resources. When looking for the means, it often pays to brainstorm a bit. Dream, then pull it back to reality.

Problem: Pat needs to learn to do auto repairs. He bombed out at school, so he can't go that route. What can he do? (Come up with at least three possibilities.)

Julie was raped when she was twelve. She now avoids and fears men. Find three possible means of overcoming this problem.

6. Evaluation:

The log system we use at Kaleidoscope includes a code and a narrative. The code is a set of symbols entered in the left-hand column which indicates the type of event recorded. In a larger area, to the right, the event can be described in detail.

The code allows us to take data on the events according to whether or not they occurred that day. Over a period of time, we can graph these events and determine their progress.

Regular progress reports give us further measure of progress according to the treatment goals and objectives. (See the attached forms for a clearer idea of these forms and how they are used.)

Subjective evaluations are also important. Feelings are significant. If the child seems calmer or more assertive, more creative or less "paranoid," this is also important. As a matter of fact, these are the concommitant effects of achievement in the objective arena. It stands to reason that the more you achieve, the better you feel about yourself, the more confidence you have and the better at ease you are with your world.

7. Dumb Luck:

There is something very humbling about seeing our noble plans and elaborate goals not work. It is often the case that the child does well despite our best brain work. And we all see cases where the opposite is true and the child "screws up" when we can find no apparent reason.

Let's admit that human beings are largely mysterious. Our best efforts may produce no effect, and a fumbling string of goof-ups may produce outstanding success.

Looking back over hundreds of kids, the common denominator for success seems to be consistency, structure and caring. With those elements present, the treatment plan makes sense and it seems that the kid can get him or herself together. As one youngster explained his perceptions of residential placement: "When I get my head together, I can go home."

KALEIDOSCOPE

LOG SHEET

DATE	CODE	EXPLANATION	SIGNATURE
	S. P. E.	Significant Positive Event - This code is used to indicate than an unusual positive behavior was exhibited by the child. It could even be a non-behavior such as a child avoiding a fight, refusing to run away, etc.	
	P. A. P.	Physical Agression/Person - Someone hit, kicked, scratched, or otherwise hurt or attempted to injure someone physically.	
	P. A. O.	Physical Aggression/Object - Someone attempted to, or actually did, inflect damage on an inanimate object (animals and plants may be included here).	
	T	Truancy from school.	
	AWOL	Absent Without Leave - Under this classification, all incidents (other than curfew violation, truancy) are included in which the child is somewhere without permission	
	V. A.	Verbal Aggression - Any threat, excessive swearing, name calling, etc.	
	C. V.	Curfew Violation - The child is out after established curfew.	
	RULE	Rule Violation - Any violation of a rule established in the house.	
	CHORE	Refusal to do a chore.	
	INTOX.	Intoxication includes any use of liquor, drugs, glue, marijuana, aerosol, or similar intoxicating substance (or suspicion of use.	
	M.	Manipulation - Each child has a style of his/her own for manipulating people. This code, when used, must be thoroughly described.	
	S.	Stealing - or suspected stealing.	
	MED.	Medical Emergency - Any medical problem should be recorded, even faked.	

Any other events should be recorded if significant, although no code exists. If it is a recurrent behavior, a code should be developed.

* - The * indicates that something must be done. You can record medical appointments, reminders to call Nurse, Social Worker, run errands, etc. with the * as a reminder.

96

Child. s name_____

KALEIDOSCOPE

LOG SHEET

DATE	CODE	EXPLANATION	STAFF'S SIGNATURE

PROGRESS REPORT & TREATMENT REVIEW

KALEIDOSCOPE

Name: _____ Period: From _____ to _____

DOB: _____ Adm.: _____ Program: _____

PROGRESS REPORT & TREATMENT REVIEW

The purpose of this report is to provide a periodic update on the progress of an individual relative to goals, problems and general status within the program. Due to the brevity of the report, supplementary documents may be added to complete the picture.

LONG RANGE NORMALIZATION GOAL

Upon completion of the program: _____

_____

Project Date: _____

SHORT TERM GOALS

GOAL	MEANS	PROGRESS	PROJECT DATE

98

PROGRESS REPORT & TREATMENT REVIEW

Date _____

UNUSUAL INCIDENTS

Date _____

GENERAL PROGRESS

The following information covers areas not included on the first page with an emphasis upon positives, as well as perspective on the problems existing:

School/Work: _____

No Resource _____ Correspondence _____ Visit to _____ Gifts to _____ Specify: _____

_____ Other than natural family _____ phone _____ visit from _____ gifts from _____

Comments: _____

FAMILY INVOLVEMENT

MEDICAL

Problems: _____

Physical _____ Results _____
Dental _____ Results _____
Eye _____ Results _____
Hearing _____ Results _____
Other _____ Results _____

Medication(s): _____

Attachments: _____

Report by: _____ Date: _____ Client: _____ Date _____

Date _____

99

CHAPTER 10

We can all blame Superman. He and his ilk really messed up our heads. We were trained to admire him for his stupendous deeds. Leaping tall buildings with a single bound, he captured the bad guys and rescued damsels and doggies in distress. Those poor plodding policemen were too dull and limited by their organization to be really effective.

Everyone wanted to be a hero. Looking silly in long blue underwear and red cape, you decided to settle for next best—child care. You soon find out that no one wants to let you do it alone. There you are, about to leap a building in a single bound, and someone tells you you need a permit.

It isn't unusual for us idealistic heroes to curse the organization for getting in our way. It takes some time before we learn that the organization is always with us, and even longer to find out that, as things are, the organization is the means for meeting the special needs of special people.

In order to meet the needs of children who could not stay in their own homes, the Department of Health, Education and Welfare takes our tax money and matches it with money from local taxes. Then through all kinds of forms and regulations, the money finds its way to your paycheck and you can support your eating habits and be free to take care of kids.

Fine, you understand that, right? You are a genuinely neat person with ideas, talents (not to mention purity of heart), and you are good for kids. It's only right that you should receive some subsistence from somewhere to do your thing. But what about those people over there in the office who come in at 8:00 and leave at 5:00? And what about the people in the state car who come and drink coffee at the big table and talk for hours? Are they necessary?

"It must be nice," you think as you try to defend yourself from the slings and arrows of outrageous children. It must be nice to sit in an air conditioned office and play with paper and drink coffee.

You recognize that someone has to be in charge, but there are so many somebodies getting paid who knows how much to do or who knows what.

It's traditional. Everybody wonders what everyone else does and if what they do is necessary. The more different the roles, the more questions everyone has about the other. Unfortunately, this kind of situation lends itself to feelings of resentment and animosity.

The employees think the boss is an SOB. The boss thinks the employees are lazy. These kinds of expectations soon begin to transform each party into warring camps firing barrages of epitaphs and dirty looks across the organizational chart.

Hopefully, this kind of warfare hasn't and won't occur in your agency. But it won't come to you as a surprise that sometimes in some places, the differences in labor that have to exist are irritated into festering divisions which serve no one.

So let's go back to the foundation of all of human services--people. People serve people. People who are administrators and others who get attached to the main offices are really people, too. They have some of the same motivation you do. Their roles are different, but just as essential. As one Alan Spear, Regional Director of Kaleidoscope, Inc. put it:

> Somewhere between you and the rest of the world, the administrators do their thing. They find the bucks to make the agency run, and then they keep track of them. They know the laws and statutes, the codes and regulations which this agency must follow to continue to exist. Hopefully, they know something about handling money--if they don't, you may end up short a paycheck. They ought to know something about personnel management--how to handle benefits, evaluate performance, give raises, arrange vacations, and keep folks happy in their jobs. Believe it or not, they almost certainly know something about child care--it is a rare child care administrator who got the job without working directly with kids somewhere along the line, and, in fact, most got where they are by being especially good at earlier jobs, specifically child care.

Nevertheless, there are administrators and other "office people" who never have done the job you do as a child care worker.

In fact, the kids are the better for that, because child care is a specific talent that everyone doesn't have.

And everyone isn't suited for administration and other office talents either. Ask yourself: Would you rather your paychecks were assured by a payroll accountant or a child care worker?

It is ideal that everyone in the agency understands and likes kids. But is isn't absolutely necessary, is it? It is essential that the "office people" have the skill to do their job and that allows you to do yours.

It is essential, as the administrator quoted above stated, that the leadership in the organization is well acquainted with child care regulations within which the agency must operate--or else.

The agency you work for also has its own policies based upon a philosophy of care. This philosophy extends back to the foundation of the organization. The philosophy is given flesh by the board and the administration.

The board, with its various members, approves new policies and resolves major issues which are brought to it. It is responsible to see to it that the agency keeps doing what it has been established to do.

People inhabit all these little boxes in the organizational chart in your agency. Each box has a human being who eats and sleeps, sweats and gets headaches, is impatient and has hopes for the future. They forget, get upset, bend rules (at times) and have other horrible faults. In other words, they are just like you and (sometimes) me.

1. Leaders, Leadership and Lead Feet:

At the top of your agency, over there in the administration building is the head honcho. He/she may be "The Administrator," "The Director," "The Executive Director" or whatever. It doesn't matter. His/her role is basically the same no matter what you call him/her.

He/she is the one who has to make sure that the agency works. If any monkey business goes on, he/she has to answer for it. All of the kids are his/her responsibility as far as their residence, care and treatment are concerned.

In order to handle this job, he/she hired you. Actually, depending on the size of the agency, he/she may have hired people who hired people (etc.) who hired you. This is the primary means administrators have of getting their job done. They hire competent people who get things done.

It's been said that an administrator is someone who knows less and less about more and more. That's a little exaggerated, but it isn't far from the truth. The administrator has to know enough about what is going on to ascertain that the agency is functioning as it should. He/she need not know every detail.

There is one thing the administrator must know, and that is how to administer. He/she must know how to get the job done through other people. This is a talent that is central to running an agency. The administrator who insists on doing everything and knowing every detail will probably earn a ride to the Funny Farm for Frantic Folks sooner or later.

There are two elements involved in getting other people to do the job. One is trust and the other is accountability. The administrator who can balance these elements is not only a good manager, he/she is an artist.

Trust implies that when a function is delegated, the manager lets the subordinate do it. The manager who doesn't trust is seen as a meddling busybody by the subordinates. This kills motivation.

The manager who trusts without setting some method of accountability destroys motivation in some people. They may ask, "Does he really care?" if they don't have to report at sometime or other on the tasks.

The ideal system to combine accountability and trust is the team approach, where goals are set as a team and problems and progress are evaluated as a team with the administrator or supervisor as the democratic leader of the team.

But the team approach is not always used. This can be for various reasons, including the leadership style of the administrators, the tasks to be worked on, the size of the agency and many other factors.

Leadership styles vary and are closely tied to the personality of the administrator. Some people are more directive than others. Some value interpersonal relations almost as much as achievement, while others are heavily task oriented and value efficiency and achievement more highly than anything else.

103

All of them are cost conscious. They are evaluated as much on their fiscal functioning as on their treatment programs. Administrators are held accountable for everything and are likely to do the same to those who work for them.

One of the complaints child care workers frequently have about administration is that "the boss doesn't give a damn for kids" because the pressures he/she exerts down the line are often budgetary or other non-direct care issues. From the administrator's point of view, Alan Spear states:

So there you are, working all kinds of hours, and you turn in your timecard showing all the time you spent and some administrator gets upset about it. Martyrdom complex ablaze, you wonder what you did wrong. Remember this—budgets are based on expected expenditures. If your agency expects to pay Child Care Workers for sixty hours per week not 95, and then it has to pay for 95 too many times, it goes broke and can't pay for any. (Or raises get held up, or the kids can't go on a trip, or the new furniture for your house doesn't come and won't be here until 1987.) Somewhere in all of this, somebody has to balance getting the job done with being able to pay for it, assuring that it is done legally, and documenting what happened so that outsiders (like the funding people) can come in and see that you did what you say you did—that somebody is the administrator, and they get ulcers and rashes like yours, but for different reasons.

The administrator has to take the long view. He/she has to see to it not only that good child care is done today, but that it is done tomorrow, next month and next year. I know of one administrator who nearly broke an agency by his generosity, leaving the next three years for his successor to have to play tightwad and SOB in order to save that agency from an untimely demise.

Many other horror stories can be told of frivolous administrators and supervisors who nearly brought ruin to their agencies and units by being too lenient and taking the short view rather than the long.

Usually, someone says "He/she is just protecting his/her job." Right. There's nothing wrong with that if at the same time he/she is protecting your job and thus attempting to help the agency continue to serve children. Don't we all protect our jobs?

If things go slowly, if it seems that the right decisions (your version) aren't made, it may be that there are larger issues at play. It is sometimes true that bungling occurs or that

104

decisions are made for the wrong (your version, again) reasons. But remember, there are people in those positions who are motivated by purposes similar to yours. In the final analysis, everyone wants to do the right thing because if they don't they won't be around very long.

Before we leave the topic of leadership, we should acknowledge the "loneliness factor" as I call it. We all make decisions based upon the knowledge we have. In organizations, information tends to get more general as it moves up the line until the top person who makes the biggest decisions is, in some ways, the least informed.

When you add to this problem the tendency everyone down the line has to cover or hide things, you have one of the bases for inappropriate decisionmaking. There is only one cure for this and that is honesty. It sometimes takes guts but without it, the administrator cannot make the correct decisions.

It follows, then, that the accountability system in your agency, if used, is one of the best means for assuring that it runs smoothly for all concerned. If it is avoided, the noises that come from your agency will be cacophonic not harmonic. It's up to us all.

2. PR: Filling the Sieve:

It would be really nice if the whole world just loved you and your agency. The local folks could have Child Care Day with parades and circuses. Famous people could come to give speeches praising your agency for its efforts. All child care workers would be toasted by the mayor, and the chief of police would buy the beer.

Well, it ain't that way, folks, in case you haven't noticed. Any parades are apt to be hostile citizens petitioning your removal, the speeches are not in favor of you and the mayor and chief of police have been told that your presence threatens their chances of having their jobs next year.

Everybody loves child care. "Those poor emotionally disturbed kids need a home and some dedicated soul to care for them." A nice little old lady in the town sent $5.00 to St. Vitus' Home for Curly Crazies in Vermont and signed a petition to get your agency run out of town the same day. Like everyone else, she loves child care--as long as it's somewhere else.

Some agencies have PR people. These are usually glib people who charm bucks out of foundations and gifts from the guilty

105

around Christmas time. Don't be fooled. No one person, no matter how energetic, can do all the PR that has to be done.

It's up to you, again.

What other people think of the agency is based upon the impressions they have received of it from whatever sources. You are one of those sources. Check your image, because it is the PR message here and now.

Your agency poses a threat to the community. Your presence should offer assurance. Whenever you have contact with the local people, you should recognize that you represent an agency that is attempting to provide a much needed service for the future. You are all they can see of the agency at that time and the people must see that you believe in what you are doing.

You may have complaints about the agency, but keep them within the agency. Don't give the public more reason to distrust the agency by your ill-chosen words.

Other cautions are in order when you deal with local agencies which also serve your children. Schools, in particular, pose special problems.

First of all, you should recognize that the kids your agency imported are a special burden to the local schools. They have to serve them, but they may not like it. The teachers (as a rule) will see your kids as their kids. Always assume that they are your partners in child care. After all, they are responsible for a major element of the child's growing years: Education.

When you are called to a teacher conference, listen patiently to what the teachers have to say. Recognize, too, that your child is one of many that they have to teach and manage. You are exactly like a parent in this situation, but you are also a professional. If you have some suggestions for management, offer them. Tell them how you deal with similar problems. Be both an advocate for the child and partner with the teacher.

You may not like what the teacher is doing. If it is really harmful in your opinion, your advocate role should dominate and you should (with your supervisor's support) request a staffing with the school and your agency.

Above all, be diplomatic. Teachers are people and people can have their professionalism overridden by vengeance at times. No point will be served by antagonizing anyone.

If you are dealing with the police or other legal authorities, you must have a similar attitude. If your child is in trouble with the police, you have to walk that fine line between child advocate and partner.

The police like to know you are responsive and they also like to be assured that you will do something specific to see that the problem will not happen again. Do everything you can to make their job easier.

The medical people are also your partners. They are very busy, and you should do everything you can to make their job easier. When you take a child to a medical appointment, you should be prepared to give medical history, explain any allergies, the nature of symptoms, etc. Also tell them what you expect from them. An amazing number of otherwise intelligent people just sit like blobs, making the doctor or nurse force information out of them.

There are other important people who sometimes get neglected. They are the receptionists and secretaries. Be sure to respect their roles in the offices you visit. Don't treat them as nobodies, because they aren't. They pass on the impressions you give them to the so-called "important people" you are trying to see. They are the ones who make things run smoothly. Don't gum up the works for them by missing appointments, being late, or dumping your garbage on them.

Sometimes poor PR is inevitable. One day a businessman was entering a downtown office building. The scene before his eyes really shocked him. There on the lobby floor a young man of sixteen was being held down by two grown men and a woman. He was screaming to be let up and none of them would relent.

What was he to think? Probably nothing good. In the heat of battle, the staff were unable to fully explain that the child had gone into an hysterical rage beyond control and there was no way they could let him go or he would have "trashed" ten or twelve cars and who knows what if they didn't restrain him until he regained composure.

Such incidents happen. It is important to not let them happen if possible. It may be better at times to let the child run away than to try to confront him or her where your ability to control is severely limited. It's hard to lay down rules. The child is more important than PR, but you have to decide whether the risk at that moment is worth the negative and positive results you might achieve.

The Engine Oilers

"You can shoot the administrator, but, for God's sake, don't shoot his secretary."

It is a fact, so little understood, that those people who do the clerical thing are absolutely essential to the running of any agency, be it a child care agency or Chase Manhattan Bank.

We deal in information exchange, mainly through paper. All the necessaries of running an agency pass through clerical hands. In fact, a great deal of the non-written communication does, too.

You really can shoot the administrators and, when the new one is hired, his/her secretary wil be able to get the replacement oriented and business will continue as usual. Even if the administrator is not immediately replaced, things will go on as long as the secretary and bookkeeper are still there.

Clerical people have jobs of varying interest and responsibility. Some are "just typists," as they say. Some are "just receptionists." Actually, the word "just" reflects an attitude toward the job that is negative. They have received that attitude from others. It really is what they make it.

Their jobs may be tedious at times. Typing long reports day after day does not excite most people, but where would be we without them? If one gets sick, we all feel it sooner or later.

The receptionists and phone answerers have a very delicate job: They have to be pleasant to everybody even when they have a headache or the boss just yelled at them.

There are a lot of unsung heroes in this group. They are largely unappreciated or treated like dirt. It seems only right that their roles should not be made more difficult by child care workers. True, they may not understand child care, but, then, you probably don't understand their job either.

The Real Heroes

A great change took place in Randy. He had been an obnoxious brat for a long time. He was totally resistant to everybody's efforts to reach him. Then one day, he just seemed to change for the better. He went along with the routines in school and in the cottage. Why?

Well, it happened on the day when Bud was picking up the trash cans. One of them fell out of the truck and while Bud was picking up the stuff, Randy came along and pitched in. After awhile, Randy was Bud's constant companion.

Randy could identify with Bud. The child care workers couldn't reach him, but Bud was something else. He looked useful in Randy's eyes. Bud did something that Randy could see himself doing when he grows up.

Not all maintenance people click with kids like Bud did. But such people have an impact on programs which is only noticed by its absence. If you don't get the plumbing fixed on time you yell. If things do go well, you take it for granted.

I have a friend, Clint, who was in charge of maintenance in a residential treatment facility, and he and I used to talk about the friction between child care and maintenance for hours. I really believe he understood child care worker problems better than they understood his.

As in all cases, things run better with understanding than with anger. It is true that your job is the most important in the agency, but it isn't always the most basic. You need to know that roles are interdependent. Prima Donnas don't make it.

The Care and Feeding of Everybody

It all boils down to the Golden Rule. If you want to get your way, help others get theirs. Any organization works only as well as its parts work together.

There is a time for everything. There is a time to confront and a time to acquiesce. There is a time to speak and a time to be quiet. There is always a time to understand and to support.

Controversy is the stuff that growth is made of, but it can also be the stuff that retards it. If your attitude is negative toward authority, you wil always find it has clay feet. You will find what you look for.

It is as much for your sanity as for the harmony of the agency that you fight battles that will make everyone a winner. No administrator or supervisor is eager to have you come in screaming and pounding the table, although this is preferable to secretively spreading discontent.

When something isn't right, address the issue to your immediate supervisor and expect you will receive a response even if it has to be taken up the line for the answer.

Remember, sometimes the answer may not suit you. On the other hand, child care workers have changed things in agencies before.

Every agency has a grievance procedure which should be used. Find out about it and use it when you need to.

A word about love. Remember, you don't have to love your boss. You may be convinced that you can do a better job, but the fact is that his/her job is partly made up of your performance. No one is a leader unless someone follows. Followership is part of leadership. Any employee can undermine a superior if he wants.

Of course, there are supervisors and administrators who should be put to pasture. The purpose of this chapter is not to deny that, but to advise you not to immediately assume that either. Proceed in good faith, and someday you may be in the driver's seat and pass this chapter on to others.

It's up to you.